THE SEVEN CHOCOLATE SINS

From Ralph
+ Sandy

THE SEVEN CHOCOLATE SINS

A Devilishly Delicious Collection of Chocolate Recipes

Ruth Moorman & Lalla Williams

QUAIL RIDGE PRESS

*Lovingly dedicated to our new daughters,
Bonnie, Pam, and Betsy*

Other books by
Ruth Moorman and Lalla Williams

**The Twelve Days of Christmas Cookbook
A Salad A Day**

Copyright © 1979 by
QUAIL RIDGE PRESS, INC.
ISBN 0-937552-01-1
Manufactured in the United States of America
First Printing, October 1979
Second Printing, April 1980
Third Printing, November 1980
Fourth Printing, June 1982
Fifth Printing, May 1985
Sixth Printing, August 1987
Book design by Barney McKee and Gwen McKee

CONTENTS

Preface 7
Lust/Candy 9
Gluttony/Pastry 17
Greed/Cookies. 29
Anger/Ice Cream 37
Envy/Cakes 45
Sloth/Puddings 61
Pride/Beverages 71
Index 77

PREFACE

Chocolate has been associated with sin for a long time--ever since "Devil's-Food Cake" first appeared on the table. And many people think that anything as good as chocolate must be sinful.

It is indeed true that there are chocoholics who *lust* after chocolate candy, *envy* their neighbor's beautiful, satiny chocolate cake, and become *gluttonous* when left alone with a dish of warm fudge pie. Some are as *proud* as "Chocolate Milk Punch" while others get *greedy* for more than just a couple of chocolaty cookies. Beware chocolate lovers! If you eat too much "Sell-Your-Soul Pudding," you will be *slothful*! And if all these devilish delights tempt you beyond resistance, cool your *anger* with "Frozen Fire" ice cream.

The Seven Chocolate Sins will attempt to prove that not everything chocolate is sinful nor every chocoholic unredeemed by offering such celestial treats as "Angel Pie" and "Bishop's Bread." In each section there are items of redemption named for saints or clergy or other inhabitants of heaven. And making its first appearance in the world of chocolate is "Seventh Heaven," a concoction of *seven* sumptious forms of chocolate!

But alas, true chocolate lovers never worry about their chocolate sins. Rather they are concerned only with keeping their blood-chocolate at a safe level, and for them this book is an invaluable aid to health! Regarding the possible caloric content of any of these recipes, we leave the reader with a final admonition--"Where ignorance is bliss, 'tis folly to be wise."

Ruth Moorman and Lalla Williams

LUST

Candy

Have you ever lusted in the depths of your dark sweet chocolate heart for a piece of scrumptious chocolate candy? Soothe such yearnings with *Heavenly Happening* or *Chocolate Persuasion Pralines.* In this section you will find such lust-satisfying delights as *Beelzebub's Baubles, Little Devils,* and *Pitch Fork Fudge. Foolish Virgins* will gorge on white chocolate fudge; wise ones will choose *Almost Divinity.*

Almost Divinity
Heavenly Happening
Chocolate Persuasion Pralines
Pitch Fork Fudge
Bitter Sweet Fruit
Beelzebub's Baubles
Parish House Fudge
Foolish Virgins
Hershey Bar Fudge
Rich Man's Fudge
Fudge Francesca
Charon's Reward
Cerberus' Chews
White Rings 'n Things
British Sins
Cool Turkish Delight
John Minary's Tranquilizers
Little Devils
Imps
Chocolate Yule Log

ALMOST DIVINITY

2 cups sugar
¾ cup corn syrup
½ cup water
¼ teaspoon salt
2 egg whites, stiffly beaten

1 teaspoon vanilla
2 ounces unsweetened chocolate, melted
1 cup pecans, chopped

Combine sugar, syrup, water and salt, and cook to hard-boil stage (255 degrees) over low heat. Beat slowly into egg whites and continue to beat until stiff. Fold in vanilla, chocolate and pecans. Drop by spoonfuls onto buttered waxed paper. Makes about 2 dozen.

HEAVENLY HAPPENING

16 ounces milk chocolate
1 tablespoon butter
Dash salt

Few drops vanilla
2 cups marshmallows, cut up
1½ cups pecans, chopped

Melt chocolate and butter in double boiler very slowly (water not boiling). Stir in salt and vanilla. Pour half the chocolate into a greased 8½ x 12½-inch Pyrex dish. Sprinkle marshmallows and nuts over chocolate. Pour on remaining half and cool. Break into pieces.

CHOCOLATE PERSUASION PRALINES

1 cup sugar
1 cup brown sugar, firmly packed
½ cup light cream
Dash salt
2 tablespoons butter

2 ounces unsweetened chocolate, melted
1 teaspoon vanilla
1 cup pecan halves

Combine sugars, cream and salt, and boil to thread stage (265 degrees) stirring occasionally. Blend in chocolate, butter, vanilla and pecan halves. Cook until soft ball stage (238 degrees). Cool and beat until slightly thickened. Drop by tablespoons onto double thickness of waxed paper.

PITCH FORK FUDGE

1 cup sugar
1 cup brown sugar, firmly packed
¾ cup milk
2 ounces unsweetened chocolate
2 tablespoons corn syrup

¼ teaspoon salt
¾ cup peanut butter
2 tablespoons butter
1 teaspoon vanilla

Combine sugars, milk, chocolate, corn syrup and salt. Cook over low heat, stirring often, until soft ball stage (238 degrees). Remove from heat. Stir in peanut butter and butter. Cool to lukewarm (110 degrees) and add vanilla. Beat until shiny smooth, then pour into buttered 9-inch square pan. Cool and cut into squares. About 4 dozen pieces.

BITTER SWEET FRUIT

1 dozen well-drained pineapple chunks
1 dozen well-drained maraschino cherries or fresh strawberries

8 ounces semi-sweet chocolate
4 tablespoons butter
1 (2-inch) square paraffin wax
1 teaspoon vanilla

Place chocolate, butter and wax in a pan over warm to very warm water. Stir until well blended. Add one teaspoon vanilla. Dip the fruit into the chocolate mixture and place on waxed paper to drain.

BEELZEBUB'S BAUBLES

2 cups molasses
1 cup cream
1 cup brown sugar, firmly packed
5 tablespoons butter

4 ounces unsweetened chocolate, melted
1 teaspoon vanilla

Boil molasses, cream, sugar and butter until firm ball stage (265 degrees). Blend in chocolate and vanilla. Pour into lightly oiled pan and cool. Mark into small squares and cut.

PARISH HOUSE FUDGE

3 cups sugar
¾ cup cocoa
1½ cups milk
4 tablespoons butter

4 ounces German sweet chocolate
2 teaspoons vanilla
1½ cups nuts, chopped

Combine sugar and cocoa in a heavy saucepan taking care to remove all lumps. Stir in milk to a smooth consistency. Cook over low heat to softball stage, stirring frequently. Remove from heat and add butter, melted chocolate and vanilla. Allow to cool and then beat until thickened. Add nuts and pour onto buttered platter. When set, cut into squares.

FOOLISH VIRGINS

1¼ cups sugar
½ cup milk
¼ teaspoon salt
3 ounces white chocolate

2 tablespoons butter
1 teaspoon vanilla
¾ cup pecans, chopped
6 ounces chocolate chips

Combine sugar, milk and salt. Boil to soft ball stage (238 degrees). Remove from heat and beat in white chocolate, butter and vanilla. Fold in nuts, then chocolate chips. Pour onto buttered dish and cut into squares.

HERSHEY BAR FUDGE

1¾ cups sugar
¼ cup brown sugar, firmly packed
3 tablespoons cocoa
¾ cups evaporated milk

¼ teaspoon salt
3 (1.5-ounce) Hershey candy bars
2 tablespoons butter
1 teaspoon vanilla

Combine and boil sugars, cocoa, milk and salt for three minutes, stirring often. Remove from heat. Blend in candy bars, butter and vanilla. Cool to lukewarm (110 degrees), and beat until thickened. Pour into buttered 9-inch square pan. Cut into squares when set.

RICH MAN'S FUDGE

2½ cups sugar
½ cup brown sugar, firmly packed
¾ stick butter
1 cup evaporated milk
¼ teaspoon salt
7 ounces semi-sweet chocolate, melted
1 ounce unsweetened chocolate, melted
2 cups marshmallow cream
½ teaspoon vanilla
2 cups pecans
White Chocolate Dip

Combine sugars, butter, milk and salt and bring to soft ball stage (238 degrees), stirring often. Remove from heat; blend in chocolates, marshmallow cream, vanilla and pecans. Pour into buttered 9 x 13-inch pan. When firm cut into squares and dip in *White Chocolate Dip.*

WHITE CHOCOLATE DIP

8 ounces white chocolate
2 tablespoons butter

Melt ingredients together in a double boiler, water not boiling, and remove from heat. Blend thoroughly and cool slightly. Dip quickly and place on waxed paper to set.

FUDGE FRANCESCA

1½ cups sugar
2½ tablespoons cocoa
5½ ounces evaporated milk
1 teaspoon corn syrup
4 tablespoons butter
1 teaspoon vanilla
1 cup pecans or walnuts, chopped

Combine sugar, cocoa, milk and corn syrup and cook to soft ball stage (238 degrees). Remove from heat and beat in butter and vanilla. Fold in nuts and pour onto greased plate to cool and harden.

Lust/Candy

CHARON'S REWARD

1¾ cups sugar
¾ cup whipping cream
¾ cup whole milk
3 tablespoons white corn syrup
Pinch of salt

1 teaspoon vanilla
½ teaspoon almond extract
1 cup almonds, chopped
Chocolate for dipping

Place sugar, cream, milk, syrup and salt into heavy saucepan. Stir and cook to soft ball stage. Remove from heat and allow to cool. Add flavorings Beat until rich and creamy, then add nuts. Pour into buttered pan. Cut into squares when cool. Prepare the chocolate for dipping as for *Bitter Sweet Fruit*. Dip each piece of candy into the chocolate, remove and place on waxed paper. When the chocolate is hardened, candy may be stored in a container.

CERBERUS' CHEWS

6 ounces semi-sweet chocolate
4 tablespoons butter
1 tablespoon water
¼ cup white corn syrup

1 tablespoon maple extract
2½ cups cereal flakes
¾ cup chopped nuts

Melt chocolate and butter in double boiler. Remove from heat and add water, syrup and maple extract. Blend well. Fold in cereal and nuts. Drop by teaspoonfuls onto waxed paper. Chill until firm.

WHITE RINGS 'N THINGS

4 oranges
2 lemons
2 limes
1½ cups water

½ cup plus 2 tablespoons sugar
Dates, pecans, pretzel bows, Chex cereal, dates stuffed with pecan halves

Cut fruit into thin slices (about ¼-inch). Remove pulp and membranes. Combine water and sugar and heat until sugar dissolves. Add fruit rings and simmer till tender. Cool. Dip rings and other "things" in *White Chocolate Dip*.

BRITISH SINS

8 ounces almonds, ground
1¾ cups powdered sugar
1 large egg white, lightly beaten
Few drops vanilla
2 tablespoons rum plus 3 drops
almond extract, or 1¼ tablespoons Amaretto
1½ teaspoons lemon juice
1½ ounces semi-sweet chocolate, grated, or chocolate for dipping

Mix together thoroughly almonds and sugar. Beat flavorings into egg white. Stir in lemon juice. Make a well in the center of the sugar mixture and add egg white. Combine thoroughly until smooth. Chill. Form into one-inch balls and roll in grated chocolate or dip in chocolate used for *Bitter Sweet Fruit.* For food processor: Process almonds with blade. Add remaining ingredients except chocolate and process until smooth.

COOL TURKISH DELIGHT

1 tablespoon gelatin
¼ cup cold water
1 cup sugar
½ cup hot water
¼ teaspoon peppermint extract or
1 tablespoon creme de menthe
Green food coloring
½ cup powdered sugar
2 tablespoons cocoa

Soften gelatin in ¼ cup cold water. Heat, stirring, sugar and hot water until sugar is dissolved. Add gelatin and boil mixture 5 minutes. Remove from heat. Add flavoring and coloring. Pour into 8-inch square pan that has been rinsed in cold water. Chill. When firm, cut into squares and dust with powdered sugar sieved with cocoa.

JOHN MINARY'S TRANQUILIZERS

16 caramels
2 tablespoons milk
16 ounces milk chocolate
1 tablespoon butter
1¼ cups salted peanuts
¾ cup marshmallow cream

Melt caramels in milk over low heat. Melt chocolate and butter in double boiler (water not boiling). Place 12 paper baking cups in muffin tins. Spoon in a little chocolate, sprinkle peanuts, then a spoonful of caramel, spoonful of marshmallow cream, spoonful of peanuts and cover with chocolate. Chill thoroughly. Addictive!

LITTLE DEVILS

6 cups powdered sugar
2 cups smooth peanut butter
1 stick butter, softened

2 teaspoons vanilla
6 ounces semi-sweet chocolate

Blend together thoroughly sugar, peanut butter, butter and vanilla. Chill. Melt chocolate in double boiler. Form peanut butter mixture into one-inch balls and dip in chocolate.

IMPS

8 ounces semi-sweet chocolate
¼ cup boiling water
1 stick sweet butter, chilled

3 tablespoons Kahlua, rum or any liqueur
¼ cup cocoa

Melt chocolate in water in double boiler. Remove from heat and beat until smooth. Gradually beat in butter which has been cut into slices. Beat in Kahlua. Chill until firm. Form one-inch balls and roll in cocoa. Refrigerate or freeze.

CHOCOLATE YULE LOG

6 ounces chocolate chips
½ cup condensed milk
½ teaspoon strong coffee, Kahlua, or Amaretto

½ teaspoon vanilla
½ cup pecans, chopped
1 egg white, slightly beaten
½ cup grated coconut

Melt chocolate in condensed milk. Stir in coffee (or liqueur), vanilla and nuts. Chill until firm enough to handle. Place on waxed paper and shape into a roll about 12 inches long. Roll up in the paper to even out the shaping. Unroll the paper and brush the mixture with egg white and press in grated coconut. Rewrap and chill until ready to cut. Keep refrigerated.

GLUTTONY
Pastry

Normal, everyday, chocolate-loving people suddenly turn into rabid gluttons when left alone with a plate of fresh chocolate doughnuts or a warm fudge pie. We balanced *Black Demon Pie* with *Meringue St. Pamela*, and *Crêpes Lucifer* with *Bishop's Bread*. And somewhere in between, there are *Crooked Halos*. In deference to those who intend to mend their gluttonous ways, there is a yogurt pie ambiguously named *Good Intentions*!

Fudge Pie
Black Demon Pie
Ginger Snap Crust
Angel Pie
Chocolate Cream Pie
Boston Cream Pie
Ciacco's Choco-Mocha Pie
Billionaire Pie
Chocolate Chess Pie
Grasshopper Pie
Graham Cracker Crust
Black Forest Pie
Chocolate Pie Crust
Hershey Bar Pie

Hershey Bar Crust
Scarlett's Pecan Pie
Angel Puffs and Eclairs
Meringue St. Pamela
Good Intentions Pie
Chocolate Wafer Crust
Creation Coffee Cake
Persian Pastries
Crêpes Lucifer
Bishop's Bread
Crooked Halos
Double Trouble Waffles
Pandora's Boxes

FUDGE PIE

1 (9-inch) pie shell, unbaked
1 stick butter, softened
1¼ cups sugar
¼ cup brown sugar, firmly packed
4 eggs
2 tablespoons corn syrup
3 ounces baking chocolate, melted
¼ teaspoon salt
1 teaspoon vanilla

Cream butter and sugar. Beat in eggs. Blend in syrup, chocolate, salt and vanilla. Pour into pie crust. Bake at 350 degrees about 25 minutes, or until top is crusty and filling set. Serve warm, or cold topped with ice cream.

BLACK DEMON PIE

1 Graham Cracker Crust or
  Ginger Snap Crust,
1 tablespoon gelatin
3 tablespoons cold water
½ cup sugar
1½ tablespoons cornstarch
2 cups milk, scalded
4 egg yolks, slightly beaten
1½ ounces unsweetened chocolate,
  melted
Dash of salt
1 teaspoon vanilla
4 egg whites
¼ teaspoon cream of tartar
½ cup sugar
1 tablespoon rum extract
½ pint whipping cream
2 teaspoons powdered sugar
Few drops vanilla
½ ounce semi-sweet chocolate,
  shaved

Soften gelatin in cold water. Combine sugar and cornstarch. Add a little milk to sugar mixture to make a paste. Add paste and gelatin to milk. Stir egg yolks into milk and cook in double boiler till custard thickens. Remove from heat and divide custard in half. To one half add chocolate, salt and vanilla. Blend thoroughly. Pour into crumb crust and chill. Next beat egg whites until frothy, then add cream of tartar and beat until stiff. Gradually beat in sugar. Fold meringue into second half of cooled custard. Add rum extract. When chocolate layer has begun to set, cover with rum custard and chill. Whip cream and blend in powdered sugar and vanilla. Spread over pie and sprinkle with shaved chocolate.

GINGER SNAP CRUST

1 cup ginger snap cookie crumbs
5 tablespoons melted butter

Form crust in 9-inch pie pan. Bake 8 minutes at 300 degrees.

Gluttony/Pastry

ANGEL PIE

½ cup granulated sugar
1 cup powdered sugar
5 egg whites
1 ounce semi-sweet chocolate, shaved
Pinch of baking powder
1 teaspoon vanilla
½ pint whipping cream, whipped and slightly sweetened

Sift sugars together four times. Beat whites till stiff. Add sugars gradually and beat well, making sure sugars and whites are well mixed. Add large pinch of baking powder and vanilla. Line a large pie pan with brown paper, shaping it so as to smooth out the bottom and raise sides to produce a concavity. Place in cool oven and bake 1½ hours at 300 degrees. Turn oven off and allow meringue to stay in oven for 2 hours. Remove and invert. Loosen the brown paper. Turn upright. Just before serving, fill with whipped cream. Cover top with shaved semi-sweet chocolate.

CHOCOLATE CREAM PIE

1 (11-inch) pie shell, baked
1½ cups sugar
3 tablespoons cornstarch
1 tablespoon flour
1 teaspoon salt
3 cups milk
4 egg yolks, slightly beaten
3 ounces unsweetened chocolate, melted
1½ teaspoons vanilla
4 egg whites
Dash of salt
8 tablespoons sugar

Combine sugar, cornstarch, flour and salt in saucepan. Add milk gradually and cook slowly until it begins to thicken. Add some of the hot mixture to the egg yolks, then stir together. Add chocolate and continue cooking, stirring often, till custard thickens. Add vanilla. Pour into baked pie shell and top with meringue made by beating egg whites and salt till stiff and then beating in sugar gradually. Bake at 300 degrees about 15 minutes or until meringue begins to brown. Cool before serving.

Gluttony/Pastry

BOSTON CREAM PIE

2¼ cups self-rising flour
1¼ cups sugar
1 stick butter, cut up

1 cup milk
1 teaspoon vanilla
2 eggs

Sift flour and sugar together. Add butter and ¾ cup of milk and beat for 2 minutes. Beat in rest of milk, vanilla and eggs one at a time. Continue to beat for 2 minutes. Bake in 2 greased, floured 9-inch cake pans at 350 degrees for about 25 minutes.

BOSTON CREAM FILLING

¾ cup milk
1 small egg
¼ cup sugar

2 teaspoons flour
½ teaspoon vanilla

Cook all ingredients till custard coats a wooden spoon. Use to fill between the layers of the cake thickly.

BOSTON CREAM FROSTING

¾ cup sugar
¼ cup flour
¾ cup milk
½ cup butter

1 teaspoon vanilla
2 ounces semi-sweet chocolate, melted

Combine sugar, flour and milk in heavy saucepan and cook, stirring till thickened. Remove from heat and add butter. Cool and add vanilla and chocolate. Beat with a mixer on high speed till ready to spread. Frost top and sides of cake.

CIACCO'S CHOCO-MOCHA PIE

1 Chocolate Wafer Crust
2 tablespoons instant coffee
¼ cup boiling water
2 cups marshmallows

½ teaspoon vanilla
½ pint whipping cream
1 ounce semi-sweet chocolate, shaved

Dissolve coffee in water. Melt marshmallows in coffee in double boiler. Stir in vanilla and blend thoroughly. Chill until mixture begins to thicken. Whip cream until firm and fold gently into coffee mixture. Pour into crust and top with shaved chocolate. Chill for 4 hours.

CLOUD NINE CHIFFON PIE

1 tablespoon gelatin
3 tablespoons cold water
2 cups milk
½ cup cocoa
3 egg yolks
½ cup sugar
3 tablespoons butter
Dash of salt
3 egg whites, stiffly beaten
1 Graham Cracker Crust

Soften gelatin in water. Make a paste with a little milk and the cocoa. Add paste to milk. Beat egg yolks with sugar, butter and salt. Add egg mixture to milk and cocoa and cook, stirring, in a double boiler until thickened. Add vanilla. Blend in gelatin. Cool. Fold egg whites gently into custard. Pour into pie shell. Chill.

BILLIONAIRE PIE

1 cup condensed milk
1 ounce unsweetened chocolate, melted
1 (9-ounce) container whipped topping
1 cup pecans, chopped
1 cup crushed pineapple, drained or ½ cup maraschino cherries, chopped
1 Graham Cracker Crust

Combine milk and chocolate in a double boiler and cook, stirring, until smooth. Cool. Fold in whipped topping, pecans and fruit. Pour into crust and chill.

CHOCOLATE CHESS PIE

1 unbaked pie shell
1½ cups sugar
2 tablespoons cocoa
1 tablespoon flour
½ teaspoon salt
1 stick butter, melted and hot
3 eggs
¼ cup warm milk
1 teaspoon vanilla
¼ teaspoon almond extract

Combine sugar, cocoa, flour, salt and mix into hot butter. Beat in eggs one at a time. Stir in milk and flavorings. Pour into pie shell and bake at 350 degrees for about 40 minutes.

GRASSHOPPER PIE

1 Graham Cracker Crust, baked
2 sticks butter
1 cup powdered sugar
2 ounces semi-sweet chocolate, melted and cooled
2 eggs, slightly beaten
½ teaspoon vanilla
½ jigger crème de cacao
½ jigger crème de menthe
½ pint whipping cream
1 tablespoon powdered sugar
1 ounce semi-sweet chocolate, shaved

Cream butter and sugar together and add chocolate. Add eggs and beat until mixture is light and fluffy. Fold in vanilla and liqueurs. Pour into pie shell, and top with whipping cream whipped with 1 tablespoon powdered sugar. Chill overnight. Before serving, top with shaved chocolate.

GRAHAM CRACKER CRUST

1 cup graham cracker crumbs
2 tablespoons sugar
4 tablespoons melted butter

Mix ingredients and press into 9-inch pie pan. Bake about 8 minutes at 300 degrees.

BLACK FOREST PIE

1 double Chocolate Pie Crust, unbaked
1 cup sugar
1 cup cherry juice
1 tablespoon tapioca
Dash of salt
¼ stick butter
½ teaspoon almond extract
2½ cups canned tart cherries, drained

Boil sugar, cherry juice, tapioca and salt for 7 minutes. Stir in butter till melted. Add flavoring and cherries. Pour filling into pie shell, cover with top crust and bake 15 minutes at 425 degrees, then about 45 minutes at 350 degrees. Serve topped with chocolate or vanilla ice cream, if desired.

Gluttony/Pastry

CHOCOLATE PIE CRUST

1 stick butter
2 cups flour
¼ teaspoon salt
6 ounces German sweet chocolate

2 tablespoons sugar
6 tablespoons water
1 teaspoon vanilla

Cut butter into flour and salt. In heavy saucepan, combine chocolate, sugar and water and cook over low heat, stirring till smooth. Add vanilla and cool. Blend into flour mixture. Makes 2 single crusts. If used as a single crust, bake for about 5 mintues at 425 degrees. For a double crust pie, bake for 15 minutes at 425 degrees, then 40 minutes at 350 degrees.

HERSHEY BAR PIE

1 (8-ounce) Hershey Bar
16 marshmallows
½ cup milk

¼ teaspoon vanilla
½ pint whipping cream

Melt chocolate bar and marshmallows in milk in double boiler. Add vanilla and cool. Whip cream until stiff and fold gently into candy mixture. Pour into crust and chill thoroughly.

HERSHEY BAR CRUST

2 (1.5-ounce) Hershey Bars
1 tablespoon butter

1 cup graham cracker crumbs

Melt Hershey Bars and butter in double boiler. Combine crumbs with melted chocolate and press into 9-inch pie pan. Bake 2 to 3 minutes at 375 degrees.

SCARLETT'S PECAN PIE

1 (9-inch) pie shell, unbaked
2 tablespoons butter, softened
1 cup sugar
3 eggs
1 cup dark syrup

2 ounces semi-sweet chocolate, melted
Dash of salt
1 teaspoon vanilla
1 cup pecan halves

Cream butter and sugar. Beat in eggs, one at a time. Blend in syrup, chocolate, salt and vanilla. Pour into crust. Arrange pecan halves on top of pie. Bake 45 minutes at 350 degrees.

Gluttony/Pastry

ANGEL PUFFS AND ECLAIRS

1 stick butter
1 cup water
Dash of salt
1 cup flour

4 eggs
½ pint whipping cream, whipped
½ recipe for Chocolate Custard
½ recipe Chocolate Butter Frosting

Bring butter, water and salt to a boil. Add flour all at once and mix thoroughly. Cook, stirring, a few minutes over low heat till mixture leaves sides of pan. Cool slightly. Beat in eggs one at a time. Continue beating until shiny smooth. Bake on greased cookie sheet--spoonfuls for puffs, finger lengths for eclairs, for 12 minutes at 450 degrees, then 20-25 minutes at 375 degrees. When cool, split and fill with custard with whipped cream folded in. Dust tops with powdered sugar. For èclairs, fill with ½ recipe for *Custard Sans Chocolate* with whipped cream folded in. Frost with *Chocolate Butter Frosting.*

MERINGUE ST. PAMELA

2 egg whites, room temperature
Dash of salt

½ cup plus 1 tablespoon sugar
¼ teaspoon vanilla

Beat the egg whites with salt until stiff but not dry. Continue beating, adding sugar gradually until mixture is very thick. Add vanilla. Pour onto greased plate and with a spatula form a ridge around the edge. Bake at 275 degrees for 1 hour or more, until thoroughly dry.

ST. PAMELA FILLING

4 egg yolks, beaten till light
3 ounces semi-sweet chocolate, melted
½ cup sugar
1 tablespoon cornstarch

Dash of salt
½ cup milk
1 teaspoon vanilla
½ pint whipping cream, whipped

In double boiler, combine egg yolks and chocolate. Combine sugar, cornstarch and salt and add to chocolate mixture. Blend in milk and cook, stirring often until thick and smooth. Remove from heat and add vanilla. Cool and pour into meringue shell. Top with whipped cream.

GOOD INTENTIONS PIE

1 Chocolate Wafer Crust
1 (3½-ounce) package instant vanilla pudding
1¾ cups milk
1 cup strawberry or raspberry yogurt
1 tablespoon strawberry or raspberry jam
1 (9-ounce) container whipped topping
½ ounce semi-sweet chocolate, shaved

Prepare instant pudding with milk. Thoroughly blend yogurt and jam into pudding. Fold in whipped topping. Pour into crust, top with chocolate, and chill 4 hours. May be frozen.

CHOCOLATE WAFER CRUST

1 cup chocolate wafer crumbs (18 Famous Chocolate Wafers)
3 tablespoons butter, melted

Mix crumbs and butter and press into 9-inch pie pan. Bake about 5 minutes in 350-degree oven.

Gluttony/Pastry

CREATION COFFEE CAKE

¼ cup shortening
1¾ cups self-rising flour
6 tablespoons sugar
2 eggs, slightly beaten

2 tablespoons oil
2 ounces semi-sweet chocolate, melted
½ cup plus 2 tablespoons milk

Cut shortening into flour. Add and stir lightly sugar, eggs, oil, chocolate and milk. Pour into greased 9-inch cake pan. Sprinkle on topping and bake 20-30 minutes at 400 degrees.

CREATION TOPPING

5 tablespoons brown sugar
5 tablespoons flour
2 tablespoons butter

½ teaspoon cinnamon
1 cup nuts, chopped

Combine sugar, flour, butter, cinnamon and nuts till mixture is uniformly crumbly.

PERSIAN PASTRIES

2 cups dried apricots
2 cups water
3 cups flour
3 tablespoons powdered sugar
1½ cups plus 2 tablespoons sugar
½ teaspoon salt
2 sticks butter

½ cup warm milk
1 package dry yeast
1 egg, slightly beaten
2 ounces semi-sweet chocolate, melted
1 teaspoon vanilla

Cook apricots in water and sugar till tender. Sift together flour, powdered sugar and salt. Cut in butter. Dissolve yeast in warm milk. Mix egg into milk. Blend in cooled chocolate. Add vanilla. Add milk mixture to flour mixture and stir until dampened. Roll out pastry very thin. Cut into 2-inch squares. Put ½ teaspoon apricots in center. Fold over and pinch corners. Bake on greased baking sheet about 15 minutes at 400 degrees. Dust with powdered sugar.

CREPES LUCIFER

1 cup flour
¼ teaspoon salt
2 eggs
1 egg yolk

½ cup milk
¼ cup water
2 tablespoons butter, melted

Combine flour, salt and eggs. Gradually stir in milk and water. Beat until smooth. Chill for ½ hour. Heat crêpe pan until very hot and brush with melted butter. Pour batter to form a very thin layer. Cook until golden brown and then cook other side. Makes 6.

LUCIFER FILLING

8 ounces cream cheese, softened
2 ounces semi-sweet chocolate, melted

2 to 3 teaspoons milk
3 tablespoons powdered sugar

Whip together cheese, chocolate, sugar and enough milk to make fluffy filling. Spoon filling in crepes, roll, and serve with *Flaming Lucifer Sauce.*

FLAMING LUCIFER SAUCE

1 stick butter
4 tablespoons sugar
½ teaspoon cornstarch

6 tablespoons water
¼ cup crème de cacao
2 tablespoons brandy or rum

Combine butter, sugar, cornstarch and water in large skillet and heat, stirring, over low heat until butter melts. Add 3 tablespoons crème de cacao and simmer 5 minutes. Carefully place crepes in sauce and heat for a minute or two. Remove crepes and add remaining creme de cacao and brandy or rum. Ignite and pour over crepes.

BISHOP'S BREAD

2 cups self-rising flour
1 cup sugar
¼ cup butter
2 eggs, well beaten
¾ cup milk

6 ounces chocolate chips
¾ cups nuts, chopped
½ cup raisins
½ cup maraschino cherries, drained and chopped

Combine flour and sugar. Cut in butter. Mix eggs and milk. Add milk to flour mixture and stir just enough to dampen. Fold in chocolate chips, nuts, raisins and cherries. Bake in a greased, floured loaf pan at 350 degrees for 1 hour, or until golden brown.

Gluttony/Pastry

CROOKED HALOS

3¾ cups self-rising flour
¼ teaspoon cinnamon
1¼ cups sugar
2 eggs, slightly beaten
3 tablespoons butter, melted

1½ ounces unsweetened chocolate, melted
1 teaspoon vanilla
1 cup milk

Combine flour and cinnamon and set aside. Beat sugar into eggs, then beat in cooled chocolate, butter and vanilla. Lightly stir in flour alternately with milk. Roll on floured board to ¼-inch thickness and cut with floured doughnut cutter. Fry, turning often, in deep fat (360-370 degrees) 2 to 3 minutes, or until lightly browned. Drain on paper towels. Glaze with *Chocolate Glaze*. Makes about 2½ dozen.

DOUBLE TROUBLE WAFFLES

2 eggs
2 tablespoons oil
1½ cups milk
1½ cups flour
2 teaspoons baking powder
½ teaspoon salt

½ cup sugar
1 teaspoon vanilla
2 ounces semi-sweet chocolate, melted
¼ cup finely chopped pecans

Mix all ingredients in processor or blender. Pour into heated waffle iron. Serve with scoop of vanilla ice cream topped with chocolate syrup.

PANDORA'S BOXES

1 package yeast
3 tablespoons warm, not hot, water
½ cup milk, scalded
2 tablespoons shortening
¼ cup sugar
½ teaspoon salt

2 eggs, slightly beaten
2 ounces semi-sweet chocolate, melted
2½ cups flour
½ recipe *Custard Sans Chocolate*

Soften yeast in warm water. Pour milk into mixer bowl. Add shortening, sugar, salt, eggs and softened yeast in order. Mix well. Blend in chocolate. Add 1 cup flour and beat thoroughly. Gradually beat in rest of flour. Let rise until about doubled. Roll out to ½-inch thickness. Cut into 2-inch squares and let rise till doubled. Fry in hot, deep fat (360-370 degrees) for 2-3 minutes. Drain on paper towels. Split and fill center with *Custard Sans Chocolate*.

GREED
Cookies

Greed (avarice) is the feeling you get when you are eating a scrumptious chocolaty cookie you want more of. Here are some we have concocted that appear to have produced just that to-be-dreaded greedy desire. But greed can lead to other sins, so beware before you find yourself at the very pit of *Dante's Inferno*, Caena, where all is ice. *Caena Cookies* are, naturally, refrigerator cookies and can be frozen. There are some lovely ladies represented here who will never have to tread the downward way.

Neglected Nuggets
Gambler's Chips
Pegged Stage Planks
Jan's Sin Squares
Forbidden Kisses
Cocoacoons
Bonnie Brownies
Top Hats
Snap Judgments
Cleopatras

Caena Cookies
Peanut Butter Hexes
Gwen's Health Food
Beatrice's Fingers
Lazy Day Cookies
Spanish Squares
Sirens
Near Fatal Drops
Chocolate Styx
Chocolate Wings

NEGLECTED NUGGETS

2 egg whites
1 teaspoon salt
¾ cup sugar
¼ teaspoon vanilla

½ teaspoon almond, mint or rum extract
12 ounces chocolate chips
½ cup coconut

Add salt to egg whites and beat until stiff. Continue beating adding sugar gradually. Beat in flavoring. Fold in the chocolate chips and coconut. Drop by spoonfuls onto ungreased cookie sheet. Place in 375-degree oven and turn off heat. Leave in oven 4 hours or overnight.

GAMBLER'S CHIPS

1 stick butter
¼ cup powdered sugar
1 ounce semi-sweet chocolate, melted

Scant 1 cup flour
Dash salt
½ teaspoon vanilla

Cream butter and sugar. Blend in chocolate and flour. Stir in salt and vanilla. Place spoonfuls on greased baking sheet and bake for about 12 minutes at 375 degrees. When cool, sandwich together with filling.

GAMBLER'S FILLING

¼ cup powdered sugar
Few drops vanilla

2 ounces semi-sweet chocolate
2 tablespoons butter

Melt chocolate and butter in double boiler. Beat in sugar. Add vanilla.

PEGGED STAGE PLANKS

1 egg
1 tablespoon milk
1 teaspoon vanilla
¾ cup sugar

¼ cup brown sugar, firmly packed
1½ cups biscuit mix
¾ cup pecans, chopped
6 ounces chocolate chips

Beat egg with milk and vanilla. Beat in sugars. Blend in--do not beat--biscuit mix, nuts and chocolate chips. Bake in a greased 9-inch square pan for 25 minutes at 350 degrees. Cool and cut into bars.

JAN'S SIN SQUARES

1 box yellow cake mix, or 2 cups self-rising flour, 1¼ cups sugar and 1 stick butter
1 stick butter, melted
1 egg, beaten
1 teaspoon vanilla

6 tablespoons cocoa
6 tablespoons boiling water
8 ounces cream cheese
3 eggs
1 box powdered sugar
1 teaspoon vanilla

Process in food processor flour, sugar and 1 stick butter till thoroughly mixed, or you may use a cake mix in place of these three ingredients if you do not have a food processor. Add and blend in butter, egg and 1 teaspoon vanilla. Press into 9 x 17-inch pan to form crust. Make a paste of the cocoa and water. Cream the cheese adding eggs one at a time. Beat in sugar. Blend in cocoa paste and vanilla. Bake 40-45 minutes at 350 degrees.

FORBIDDEN KISSES

4 egg whites
¼ teaspoon salt
1 cup plus 2 tablespoons sugar
4 tablespoons cocoa

¼ teaspoon vanilla
1 cup whipping cream
1 tablespoon powdered sugar

Beat egg whites and salt until stiff but not dry. Combine sugar and cocoa and beat into eggs gradually. Blend in vanilla. Drop by spoonfuls onto greased baking sheet. Bake about 1 hour, or until dry, at 275 degrees. Sandwich together with cream whipped with powdered sugar.

COCOACOONS

2¼ cups flour
½ cup powdered sugar
2 tablespoons cocoa

1 cup pecans, chopped
1½ sticks butter, melted
1 teaspoon vanilla

Mix flour, sugar, cocoa and pecans. Add butter and vanilla. Roll into cocoons and bake about 45 minutes at 325 degrees.

BONNIE BROWNIES

2 sticks butter, softened
2 cups sugar
3 eggs
½ cup cocoa
1½ cups flour
1½ cups pecans, chopped
1 teaspoon vanilla

Cream butter and sugar. Add remaining ingredients, mixing well after each addition. Do not overcook. Bake in well-greased 9 x 13-inch pan at 350 degrees for 25 minutes.

INTERMEDIATE FROSTING

1 box powdered sugar
Milk
1 tablespoon white crème de menthe

Mix sugar with enough milk to make a spreading consistency. Add crème de menthe. Spread over brownies.

FINAL FROSTING

3 ounces unsweetened chocolate, melted
5 tablespoons butter, softened

Combine and pour over sugar frosting. Chill.

TOP HATS

Vanilla wafers
Marshmallows
Chocolate Butter Frosting

Put one dab of frosting in center of vanilla wafer. Place marshmallow on top and frost the entire "hat." Kids love to make and eat these!

Greed/Cookies

SNAP JUDGMENTS

1 stick butter
½ cup brown sugar, firmly packed
1 egg
1 egg yolk
½ teaspoon vanilla
1½ cups flour
½ teaspoon cinnamon
¼ teaspoon soda
¼ teaspoon salt
1 cup pecans, chopped

Cream butter and sugar. Beat in egg and egg yolk, then vanilla. Add flour, cinnamon, soda and salt and mix thoroughly. Stir in pecans. Shape into 1-inch balls and bake on a greased cookie sheet for about 12 minutes at 350 degrees. Cool and frost with *Chocolate Butter Frosting*.

CLEOPATRAS

1 stick butter
½ cup cocoa
½ cup milk
1 cup sugar
½ cup brown sugar, firmly packed
2 cups flour
1 teaspoon salt
½ teaspoon cinnamon
3 eggs, beaten
½ cup corn syrup
1 teaspoon vanilla
1½ cups dates
1½ cups pecans, chopped
½ cup raisins

Melt butter over low heat. Add cocoa and milk and heat until blended, stirring often. Combine sugars, flour, salt and cinnamon. Combine and mix thoroughly cocoa mixture, dry ingredients, eggs, corn syrup and vanilla. Fold in the fruit and nuts. Bake in a greased, floured 9 x 17-inch pan for about 30 minutes at 325 degrees. Cut into squares. Makes about 5 dozen.

CAENA COOKIES

1 stick butter, softened
8 ounces cream cheese, softened
½ cup sugar
2 ounces semi-sweet chocolate,
melted and cooled
1 teaspoon vanilla
2 cups flour
¼ teaspoon salt

Cream butter, cream cheese and sugar. Blend in chocolate and vanilla. Sift flour with salt and blend thoroughly into chocolate mixture. Shape in 2-inch rolls and wrap in waxed paper. Chill till firm. Slice about ¼-inch thick. Bake 6 minutes at 400 degrees. Cookie dough can be frozen.

PEANUT BUTTER HEXES

½ cup butter
¾ cups brown sugar, firmly packed
¼ cup white sugar
1 large egg
1 cup crunchy peanut butter

1½ cups flour
½ teaspoon salt
½ teaspoon soda
1 teaspoon vanilla
6 ounces chocolate chips

Cream butter and sugars. Add egg and beat until fluffy. Beat in peanut butter and flour mixed with salt and soda. Add vanilla. Blend in chocolate chips. Roll dough into one-inch balls. Place on greased baking sheet and press balls down with a fork making "hexes." Bake 12-15 minutes at 375 degrees. Makes about 60.

GWEN'S HEALTH FOOD

1½ cups flour
1 teaspoon baking soda
1 teaspoon salt
1 cup sugar
1 cup brown sugar, firmly packed
2 sticks butter, softened
2 eggs

1 teaspoon vanilla
3 cups oats, uncooked
½ cup pecans, chopped
6 ounces chocolate chips
¼ cup unprocessed wheat bran
¼ cup wheat germ

Sift together flour, soda and salt. Add sugars, butter, eggs and vanilla. Beat 2 minutes. Stir in oatmeal, pecans, chocolate chips, bran and wheat germ. Mixture will be stiff. Shape dough into 3 rolls, 1½ inches in diameter, and chill thoroughly. Slice about ½-inch thick. Bake on greased baking sheets 10 minutes at 350 degrees.

BEATRICE'S FINGERS

Lady Fingers
Rum, or any liqueur

Whipped cream, slightly sweetened
Hot Fudge Sauce

Split Lady Fingers, drizzle liqueur over bottom half. Sandwich together with whipped cream and top with *Hot Fudge Sauce.*

LAZY DAY COOKIES

1½ cups sugar
½ cup brown sugar, firmly packed
½ cup milk
½ stick butter
½ cup crunchy peanut butter
¼ cup coconut
1 teaspoon vanilla
6 tablespoons cocoa
3 cups quick-cooking oats

Boil sugars, milk and butter for 1 minute. Add rest of ingredients in order listed and mix thoroughly. Drop by spoonfuls onto waxed paper to harden. Makes about 5 dozen cookies. Tastes like fudge!

SPANISH SQUARES

2 sticks butter, softened
½ cup sugar
½ cup brown sugar, firmly packed
2 eggs
14 ounces caramels
¼ cup milk
2 eggs, beaten
2 cups flour
1 teaspoon baking powder
½ teaspoon soda
¼ teaspoon salt
1 teaspoon cinnamon
1 teaspoon vanilla
2 cups oats, uncooked
6 ounces chocolate chips
1 cup nuts, chopped

Cream butter and sugars. Beat in eggs. Melt caramels in milk and blend into egg mixture. Sift together flour, baking powder, soda, salt and cinnamon. Combine with egg mixture. Add vanilla, then oats. Fold in chocolate chips and nuts. Bake in greased 9 x 13-inch pan for about 15 minutes or until golden brown at 350 degrees. Cool and cut into squares.

SIRENS

3 cups self-rising flour
1 pound brown sugar
1 teaspoon cinnamon
3 eggs, slightly beaten
1¼ cups corn oil
2 teaspoons vanilla
12 ounces chocolate chips
2 cups pecans or walnuts
½ cup raisins

Combine dry ingredients. Add eggs, corn oil and vanilla and beat until thoroughly blended. Fold in chocolate chips, nuts and raisins. Bake in a greased, floured 9 x 13-inch pan at 350 degrees about 1 hour. When cool, cut into squares.

NEAR FATAL DROPS

1 stick butter
½ cup light cream
1 cup sugar
1¼ cups flour
¼ teaspoon baking powder
¼ teaspoon salt

6 ounces chocolate chips
¾ cup maraschino cherries, drained and chopped
1 cup almonds, slivered
½ teaspoon almond extract

Melt butter with cream and sugar. Cook over low heat until sugar dissolves. Sift together flour, baking powder and salt. Mix together in a bowl chocolate chips, cherries and half the flour mixture. Add the hot, melted mixture and mix well. Stir in rest of flour mixture and extract. Drop by spoonfuls onto greased cookie sheet and bake for 15-20 minutes at 325 degrees. Makes about 5 dozen.

CHOCOLATE STYX

8 cups flour
1¾ cups sugar
3½ tablespoons cocoa
6 eggs

½ cup oil
1 tablespoon anise seed
2 tablespoons baking powder

Pour out flour on a bread board and make a well in the center. Combine sugar and cocoa. Beat eggs with sugar mixture and pour into center of flour. With a fork, stir in oil, anise seed and baking powder. Stir with hand (Italian method) and knead, adding as much flour as needed to make a dough stiff enough to handle. Make 1-inch rolls. Bake at 350 degrees on greased baking sheet 15 minutes or till slightly brown. Slice diagonally. Return to oven 8-10 minutes to toast. Store in tightly covered container.

CHOCOLATE WINGS

Devil's-Food Cake
8 ounces cream cheese, softened
1 tablespoon maraschino cherry juice

1 or 2 teaspoons milk
2 tablespoons maraschino cherries, chopped

Bake *Devil's-Food Cake* in cupcakes about 20 minutes at 375 degrees. Whip cream cheese with juice and milk till fluffy. Fold in cherries. Slice top off cupcakes and cut slice in half. Spread bottom of cupcakes with cream cheese. Stand halves, slanting inward, to look like wings. ("Devil's Wings" for Halloween; "Angel's Wings" for Christmas!)

ANGER
Ice Cream

In the heat of anger, reach for a dish of ice cream to cool your temper. A few of these devilish delights combine fire with ice (cream). Some are pure chocolate, some to be topped with chocolate, some encased in chocolate. All are guaranteed to satisfy your chocolate tooth.

Chocolate Envy
Coffee Confection
Fire 'n Ice Cream
Refrigerator Ice Cream
Frozen Fire
Chocolate Sherbet
Hot Fudge Sauce
Hot Fudge Royale Sauce
Hot Stuff!
Chocolate Cases
Chocolate Syrup
Cocoa Syrup

Sunday Soda
Heaven Can Wait Pie
Blazing Bananas
Cherries Jubilee de Cacao
Tortoni Santa Lucia
Parfait Apollo
Klondike Demon
Flaming Black Forest Cake
Preacher's Dessert
Chocolate Bombe
Mint Frappé
Meringue Glacé

CHOCOLATE ENVY

1 quart light cream
1 teaspoon vanilla
1 teaspoon almond extract
¾ cup sugar
Pinch of salt

1 cup chocolate chips
1½ cups pistaschio nuts, slightly toasted
Green food coloring

Combine first 5 ingredients. Add chocolate chips which have been broken up, and the toasted nuts. Color if desired. Freeze in ice cream freezer.

COFFEE CONFECTION

1 egg beaten with 1 egg yolk
¼ cup sugar
1 tablespoon instant coffee
1 teaspoon boiling water
1 cup light cream

½ pint whipping cream, whipped slightly
2 ounces semi-sweet chocolate, shaved
3 tablespoons almonds, sliced

Cream eggs and sugar. Add coffee dissolved in boiling water. In a double boiler, heat light cream with eggs and sugar, stirring, until custard begins to thicken. Fold in slightly whipped cream, chocolate and almonds. Freeze in ice cream freezer.

FIRE'N ICE CREAM

1 quart light cream
1 tablespoon vanilla
¾ cup sugar
Dash of salt

2 ounces unsweetened chocolate, melted
½ cup hot cream

Combine first four ingredients. Slowly add chocolate to the ½ cup hot cream. Blend well and add to first mixture. Freeze in ice cream freezer.

REFRIGERATOR ICE CREAM

1 cup condensed milk
Chocolate Syrup

½ pint whipping cream, whipped
2 egg whites, stiffly beaten

Blend milk and syrup into cream. Fold in egg whites. Freeze in freezer trays.

Anger/Ice Cream

FROZEN FIRE

1 cup milk, scalded
2 eggs
½ cup sugar
1 tablespoon butter

½ pint whipping cream, whipped
Few drops peppermint extract
2 ounces semi-sweet chocolate
1 tablespoon water

Beat eggs with sugar and pour into milk. Strain into pan rinsed with cold water; add butter and cook, stirring over low heat until custard thickens. Cool. Fold cream and peppermint into custard. Pour into freezer trays and freeze until thick and creamy but not stiff. While custard is freezing (about 20 minutes), melt chocolate in water. When custard is ready, swirl chocolate through to make a rippled effect. Freeze.

CHOCOLATE SHERBET

1 quart milk
2 ounces semi-sweet chocolate, broken up

Dash of salt
1 teaspoon vanilla

Combine milk, chocolate and salt in saucepan. Stir over low heat until mixture is very smooth. Remove from heat and add vanilla. Freeze in freezer trays until firm about 1 inch from the edge. Beat with mixer or process until consistency is even. Return to freezer trays.

Anger/Ice Cream

HOT FUDGE SAUCE

2 cups sugar
1 tablespoon cocoa
Dash of salt
2 ounces unsweetened chocolate
¾ cup evaporated milk
1 tablespoon butter
1 teaspoon vanilla

Combine sugar, cocoa and salt. Add other ingredients except vanilla. Cook, stirring until chocolate melts and sugar dissolves. Boil about 5 minutes till thick. Add vanilla.

HOT FUDGE ROYALE SAUCE

1 (14-ounce) can condensed milk
2½ ounces unsweetened chocolate
Dash of salt
¾ cup hot water
½ teaspoon vanilla
1 tablespoon Kahlua

Combine condensed milk, chocolate and salt. Place in top of double boiler. Cook until thick and remove from heat. Stir in hot water, vanilla and Kahlua. Serve hot or cold over favorite dessert.

HOT STUFF!

½ cup sugar
¼ cup brown sugar, firmly packed
6 tablespoons cocoa
Dash of salt
3 tablespoons butter
1 cup light cream
1 teaspoon vanilla
¼ cup brandy
¼ cup crème de cacao

Combine sugars, cocoa, salt and butter over low heat. Stir until butter melts. Add cream and cook, stirring often, until thickened. Add vanilla. When ready to serve, warm chocolate mixture. Warm brandy and liqueur together and pour gently over chocolate. Light. Serve immediately over ice cream.

CHOCOLATE CASES

6 ounces chocolate chips
1 tablespoon butter
½ cup coconut (optional)

Melt chocolate and butter over low heat. Stir in coconut. Place 8 paper baking cups into a muffin pan and drizzle chocolate onto inner surface of cups. Chill and remove paper. Fill with ice cream or pudding.

Anger/Ice Cream

CHOCOLATE SYRUP

6 ounces unsweetened chocolate
1 (14-ounce) can condensed milk
5 tablespoons sugar
1 cup boiling water
Dash of salt
1 teaspoon vanilla

Melt chocolate in milk in double boiler. Add sugar and water and stir until sugar is dissolved. Heat until thoroughly blended. Add salt and vanilla. Store in a tightly covered jar in refrigerator. Makes 2¼ cups. Use as sauce or for a chocolate drink, 2 tablespoons per cup of milk.

COCOA SYRUP

1 cup cocoa
½ cup sugar
¾ cup corn syrup
¼ teaspoon salt
1 cup water
2 teaspoons vanilla

Combine cocoa and sugar. Add syrup, salt and water. Cook, stirring, over low heat until smooth. Boil 3 minutes, stirring constantly. Add vanilla. Cool. Store in a tightly covered jar in refrigerator. Makes 2 cups. Use as sauce or for a chocolate drink, 2 tablespoons per cup of milk.

SUNDAY SODA

2 tablespoons Chocolate Syrup
½ cup club soda
¼ cup milk
2 scoops vanilla ice cream (or 1 scoop chocolate)
Whipped cream
Maraschino cherry

Pour syrup into glass and stir in soda water. Add milk and ice cream and stir lightly. Top with whipped cream and a cherry.

HEAVEN-CAN-WAIT PIE

Chocolate Wafer Crust
1½ pints ice cream (coffee, almond, or butter pecan), softened
Hot Fudge Sauce
½ pint whipping cream, whipped and slightly sweetened

Spread ice cream on crust. Top with sauce, then whipped cream.

BLAZING BANANAS

1 pint chocolate ice cream
½ stick butter
½ cup brown sugar, firmly packed
3 bananas, peeled and cut in half lengthwise
Dash cinnamon
¼ cup crème de cacao
½ cup white rum

Spoon ice cream into six sherbet glasses. Melt butter and sugar in skillet. Sauté bananas in mixture until tender, cutting into bite-size pieces. Sprinkle with cinnamon. Pour in liqueur and rum. Remove from heat. Light. Spoon immediately over ice cream.

CHERRIES JUBILEE DE CACAO

1 tablespoon cornstarch
1 teaspoon cold water
2 tablespoons sugar
1 (16-ounce) can dark cherries, drained
Juice from cherries
½ cup brandy
¼ cup crème de cacao
Chocolate ice cream

Dissolve cornstarch in water. Add sugar and liquid drained from cherries. Cook, stirring, until thick and transparent. Pour over cherries. Add brandy and liqueur. Light. Stir as flame burns. Pour over ice cream. Serves 4-6.

TORTONI SANTA LUCIA

4 egg yolks
¾ cup sugar
2 tablespoons boiling water
1 pint whipping cream, whipped
4 egg whites
½ cup sugar
3 tablespoons instant coffee
3 tablespoons cocoa
2 teaspoons almond extract
1 teaspoon vanilla
½ cup toasted almonds, chopped

Combine yolks and ¾ cup sugar. Beat until lemon colored. Add water and blend. Fold in whipped cream. Beat whites till stiff. Combine rest of sugar, coffee and cocoa. Fold into beaten whites. Add flavorings. Beat well and fold into yolk mixture and add almonds. Spoon into paper muffin cups and freeze. Makes 2 dozen cups.

Anger/Ice Cream

PARFAIT APOLLO

½ gallon coffee ice cream
6 tablespoons crème de cacao
6 tablespoons Amaretto
1 cup whipped topping
1 tablespoon instant coffee
1 tablespoon chocolate syrup

2 tablespoons boiling water
½ cup whipping cream, unwhipped
½ pint whipping cream, whipped
   and slightly sweetened
6 maraschino cherries
6 mint sprigs

Place parfait glasses in freezer till frosted. Into each, place 2 scoops of ice cream. Combine the liqueurs and pour 2 tablespoons over each. Combine instant coffee, syrup and boiling water. Mix with cream and fold into whipped topping. Use this mixture to fill in the spaces between the scoops of ice cream so that the glass has no empty spaces. Top each with sweetened whipped cream. Garnish with a cherry and a sprig of mint.

KLONDIKE DEMON

½ recipe for Seventh Heaven Cake
   or Fudge Fantasy Cake
1 pint chocolate ice cream,

softened
Meringue from Forbidden Kisses

Spoon ice cream on cooled cake in even layer. Cover completely with meringue. Bake 8-10 minutes, or until golden, at 425 degrees.

FLAMING BLACK FOREST CAKE

½ stick butter
½ cup sugar
2 eggs
2 ounces unsweetened chocolate,
   melted
½ teaspoon vanilla

1 cup flour
1 teaspoon baking powder
¾ cup milk
2 pints vanilla ice cream, softened
1 tablespoon kirsch
Cherries Jubilee de Cacao

Cream butter and sugar. Beat in eggs, one at a time. Blend in chocolate and vanilla. Beat in alternately, flour mixed with baking powder and milk. Bake in a greased, floured 8-inch pan for about 30 minutes at 350 degrees. Cool in pan 5 minutes. Turn cake out on rack. When cool, slice into 2 layers. For ice cream layers, stir kirsch into ice cream and spread into two 8-inch cake pans lined with foil extended beyond the rim of the pan. Freeze. When ready to serve, assemble cake beginning with a cake layer, then an ice cream layer. Serve *Cherries Jubilee de Cacao* over each slice.

PREACHER'S DESSERT

6 ounces semi-sweet chocolate, melted
1½ cups marshmallows
1 cup evaporated milk
Dash of salt
1 quart vanilla ice cream
½ cup toasted pecans, chopped

Combine chocolate, marshmallows, milk and salt in heavy saucepan. Cook, stirring, until mixture thickens. Cool. Spoon chocolate into parfait glasses, then ice cream, more chocolate, and top with nuts. Serves 8.

CHOCOLATE BOMBE

Line a mold with vanilla or coffee ice cream about 1 inch thick. Fill with *Mad About Mousse.* Cover and freeze.

MINT FRAPPE

1 pint chocolate ice cream, softened
¼ cup crème de cacao
¼ cup crème de menthe
½ ounce semi-sweet chocolate, shaved

Blend or process ice cream with liqueurs. Spoon into parfait or sherbet glasses. Top with chocolate. Serve immediately. Serves 4.

MERINGUE GLACE

Meringue from Meringue St. Pamela
Chocolate ice cream
Whipped cream

Bake meringue in 3-inch rounds. Top with ice cream and whipped cream.

Anger/Ice Cream

ENVY
Cakes

Someone else's dark shiny chocolate frosted cake can inspire the cocoaest envy in the eye of the chocoholic beholder. With one of these on your own cake pedestal, you need not envy anyone since their beauty is more than frosting deep. The *Vicarage Tea Cake* recipe came from England and is unlike American cakes in that it is not so moist--definitely to be enjoyed with a "nice cuppa" tea or coffee.

Devil's-Food Cake
Fudge Fantasy Cake
Persephone's Cake
Seventh Heaven Cake
Sheer Perfidy
Vicarage Tea Cake
Chocolate Myracle
Tower of Babel Cake
German Sweet Chocolate Cake
"Looking for Mr. Goodbar" Cake
Hershey Bar Cake
Fat City
Milky Way Cake
Gateau Diabolique
Nearly Nutritious Cake
Eden Vale Cake
Fallen Angel
Chocolate Confusion
Sacher Torte
Hazel Nut Torte
Hell Week Cake

Screwtape Roll
Witches' Gold
Chocolate Pound Cake
Chocolate Chiffon Cake
Amaretto Cake
Black Forest Cake
Archangel's Cake
Black Velvet
Macaroon Cupcakes
Creamy Chocolate Frosting
Chocolate Cream Frosting
Angel Fluff Frosting
Chocolate Butter Frosting
Continental Cream Frosting
Viennese Cream Frosting
Seven-Minute Frosting
Chocolate Seven-Minute Frosting
Chocolate Glacé Frosting
Chocolate Glaze
Fudge Frosting
Country Frosting

DEVIL'S-FOOD CAKE

½ cup shortening
2 cups sugar
¾ cup cocoa
1 teaspoon instant coffee
2 large eggs

2 teaspoons soda
1¾ cups buttermilk
½ teaspoon salt
2 cups flour
2 teaspoons vanilla

Cream shortening, sugar, cocoa and coffee. Add unbeaten eggs. Stir soda into milk and set aside. Add salt to flour and fold into the cake mixture alternating with the milk. Add vanilla and bake in 350-degree oven in 2 cake pans for about 23-25 minutes. Frost with *Seven-Minute Frosting*, or for more devilish palates, any of the rich chocolate ones.

FUDGE FANTASY CAKE

1 stick butter
¼ cup sugar
1 cup brown sugar, firmly packed
2 eggs
3 ounces unsweetened chocolate, melted and cooled

1 teaspoon vanilla
2 cups cake flour
1½ teaspoons baking powder
½ teaspoon salt
½ teaspoon soda
1 cup milk

Cream butter and sugars. Beat in eggs, one at a time. Blend in chocolate and vanilla. Sift together flour, baking powder, salt and soda. Beat in flour alternately with milk. Bake in two 9-inch, greased, floured cake pans 25-30 minutes at 350 degrees. Frost with *Chocolate Cheese Frosting*. Too good to be true!

PERSEPHONE'S CAKE

2¼ cups cake flour, sifted
1½ cups sugar
¼ cup brown sugar, firmly packed
1½ teaspoons baking soda
1 teaspoon salt
1 stick butter, softened

1½ cups buttermilk
1 teaspoon vanilla
2 eggs
2 ounces unsweetened chocolate, melted

Sift together dry ingredients into large mixing bowl. Add butter, 1 cup buttermilk and vanilla. Beat 2 minutes at medium speed. Beat in eggs one at a time. Add ½ cup buttermilk and beat for 2 minutes. Bake in greased, floured 9-inch cake pans for 30 minutes at 375 degrees. Frost with *Chocolate Butter Frosting*.

SEVENTH HEAVEN CAKE

4 ounces white chocolate, shaved
1 teaspoon water
2 sticks butter, softened
2 cups cake flour
½ teaspoon salt
1 teaspoon soda
1½ cups sugar
1 cup buttermilk
2 eggs
1 teaspoon vanilla
½ cup chocolate chips
½ cup pecans, chopped
½ cup coconut
½ recipe Chocolate Custard
6 chocolate caramels
2 tablespoons crème de cacao
Chocolate sprinkles

Melt white chocolate in water over low heat. Cream butter and blend in chocolate. Sift flour with salt and soda. Add flour mixture, sugar and buttermilk. Beat 2 minutes. Beat in eggs one at a time. Add vanilla. Fold in chocolate chips, pecans and coconut. Bake in 2 well-greased, floured 9-inch cake pans about 30 minutes at 350 degrees. Add caramels to custard when custard becomes thick. Stir until caramels melt. Cool. When cake is cool, drizzle crème de cacao on bottom layer. Sandwich layers with custard. Frost with *Seventh Heaven Frosting*. Add chocolate sprinkles on top.

SEVENTH HEAVEN FROSTING

½ cup powdered sugar
1 teaspoon cocoa
½ pint whipping cream
Few drops vanilla

Combine sugar and cocoa. Whip cream till frothy. Gradually beat in sugar mixture. Add vanilla.

SHEER PERFIDY

8 (1.5-ounce) chocolate bars
1 large can chocolate syrup
2 cups sugar
2 sticks butter, softened
5 medium eggs (or 4 large)
2½ cups flour
¼ teaspoon soda
1 cup buttermilk
1 cup chopped nuts
2 teaspoons vanilla
3 tablespoons strong coffee

Melt candy in double boiler. In separate bowl, cream butter and sugar. Add eggs one at a time and mix well. Sift flour and soda together. Add, alternating with buttermilk, syrup and candy. Beat well. Add nuts, vanilla and coffee. Bake in greased tube pan 1½ hours at 350 degrees.

Envy/Cakes

VICARAGE TEA CAKE

1½ sticks butter, softened
1 cup plus 2 tablespoons sugar
2 eggs
1 cup plus 4 tablespoons self-
rising flour
4 tablespoons cocoa
4 tablespoons boiling water
1 teaspoon vanilla

Cream butter and sugar. Beat in eggs one at a time until fluffy. Add flour gradually. Make a paste with cocoa and boiling water and blend thoroughly into batter. Add vanilla. Bake in 2 buttered and floured 8-inch round cake pans for 20-25 minutes at 325 degrees. Remove from pans and cool before frosting.

VICARAGE FROSTING

4 tablespoons cocoa
4 tablespoons boiling water
2 cups powdered sugar
½ stick butter, softened
1 teaspoon vanilla

Make a paste with cocoa and boiling water. Beat all ingredients until creamy. If necessary, add a little milk, very little.

CHOCOLATE MYRACLE

1 cup water
2 sticks butter
4 tablespoons cocoa
2 cups sugar
2 cups flour
¼ teaspoon salt
2 eggs, slightly beaten
½ cup buttermilk
1 teaspoon soda
1 teaspoon vanilla

Boil water, butter and cocoa. Add to the combined sugar, flour and salt. Mix together the eggs, buttermilk, soda and vanilla. Pour into first mixture and blend well. Bake in a greased, floured 9 x 17-inch pan for about 30 minutes at 350 degrees.

MYRACLE TOPPING

1 stick butter
4 tablespoons cocoa
Dash of salt
7 tablespoons milk
1 box powdered sugar
1 teaspoon vanilla
2 cups pecans, chopped

While cake is baking, bring to a boil the butter, cocoa, salt and milk. Add the sugar and vanilla and mix well. Fold in the pecans. Pour the topping over the cake as soon as it has baked.

TOWER OF BABEL CAKE

1 cup butter, softened
2 cups sugar
4 eggs
3 cups flour

1 teaspoon baking powder
1 teaspoon salt
1 cup milk
1 teaspoon vanilla

Cream butter and sugar until creamy. Beat in eggs one at a time. Sift together flour, baking powder and salt, and add alternately with milk. Add vanilla. Bake in 7 greased, floured 9-inch cake pans for about 8 minutes at 375 degrees. Fill and frost with *Viennese Cream Frosting*.

GERMAN SWEET CHOCOLATE CAKE

2 cups sifted cake flour
1 teaspoon soda
½ teaspoon salt
1½ bars German sweet chocolate
½ cup boiling water
1 cup margarine

1¾ cups sugar
¼ cup brown sugar
4 egg yolks
1½ teaspoons vanilla
1 cup buttermilk
4 egg whites

Sift flour before measuring. Add soda and salt and sift again twice. Melt chocolate in boiling water and set aside. Cream sugars and margarine until light and fluffy. Add the egg yolks one at a time blending well after each addition. Add chocolate and vanilla. Add flour mixture alternately with buttermilk. Fold in beaten egg whites. Bake in 3 pans lined with brown paper for 35 minutes at 350 degrees. Frost with *German Sweet Chocolate Frosting* or *Continental Cream Frosting*.

GERMAN SWEET CHOCOLATE FROSTING

½ pint whipping cream
¾ cup sugar
3 egg yolks

1 stick butter
1½ teaspoons vanilla

Cook and stir the above ingredients until thickened. Allow to cool and beat until desired spreading consistency is reached. Add a cup of chopped pecans and a cup of frozen, grated coconut, if desired.

"LOOKING FOR MR. GOODBAR" CAKE

2 sticks butter, softened
1¾ cups sugar
¼ cup brown sugar, firmly packed
4 eggs
8 (1.5-ounce) Mr. Goodbar candy bars
1 ounce semi-sweet chocolate
2 tablespoons water
½ teaspoon baking soda
1 cup buttermilk
2¼ cups flour
½ teaspoon salt

Cream butter and sugars. Beat in eggs, one at a time. Melt candy bars and chocolate in water. Blend chocolate into creamed mixture. Stir soda into buttermilk. Sift together flour and salt. Add flour alternately with milk. Bake in a greased, floured tube pan 1 hour 50 minutes-2 hours at 325 degrees. Glaze with *Chocolate Glaze,* if desired. Serves a crowd!

HERSHEY BAR CAKE

10 (l.5-ounce) Hershey candy bars
2 sticks butter, 1 softened
1¾ cups sugar
4 eggs
2½ cups flour
1 cup buttermilk
½ teaspoon soda
2 teaspoons vanilla
¾ cup chopped nuts

Melt candy bars and one stick of butter and set aside. Cream sugar and softened stick butter until light and fluffy. Add eggs one at a time, beating well after each addition. Add flour, buttermilk and soda. Add melted chocolate, vanilla and chopped nuts. Bake in greased, floured tube or Bundt pan 60 minutes at 325 degrees.

HERSHEY BAR FROSTING

2 (l.5-ounce) Hershey candy bars
1 stick butter
1¾ cups powdered sugar

Melt candy bars and butter in top of double boiler. Add powdered sugar until desired thickness. If extra liquid is needed, a little unsweetened strong coffee may be added.

Envy/Cakes

FAT CITY

2 ounces semi-sweet chocolate
1 ounce unsweetened chocolate
3 tablespoons water
1 cup butter, softened
3 cups sugar

6 eggs
3 cups cake flour
¼ teaspoons soda
1 cup sour cream
1¼ teaspoons vanilla

Melt chocolate in water over low heat. Cream butter and sugar. Add eggs one at a time, beating until fluffy. Add chocolate and blend thoroughly. Mix soda in flour and add alternately with sour cream beginning and ending with flour. Add vanilla. Pour over the topping mixture and bake about 1½ hours at 300 degrees. Remove from pan as soon as baked. Cool before frosting.

FAT CITY TOPPING

4 teaspoons sugar
1 teaspoon cinnamon

1 cup pecans, coarsely chopped

Thoroughly mix the sugar, cinnamon and pecans. Put in bottom of a greased Bundt or tube pan.

FAT CITY FROSTING

5 ounces semi-sweet chocolate
3 tablespoons water
¼ cup butter, softened

8 ounces cream cheese, softened
1 box powdered sugar
2 teaspoons vanilla

Melt chocolate in water over low heat. Cream butter and cream cheese. Blend in chocolate. Beat in powdered sugar. Add vanilla.

MILKY WAY CAKE

½ pound Milky Way candy
2 sticks butter, 1 softened
1 cup sugar
1 cup brown sugar, firmly packed
4 eggs
1 ounce semi-sweet chocolate,
   melted and cooled

2¼ cups flour
½ teaspoon salt
½ teaspoon soda
1 cup buttermilk
1 teaspoon vanilla
1 cup pecans, chopped

Melt candy and 1 stick butter over low heat. Cream softened butter and sugars. Beat in eggs one at a time. Blend in chocolate. Sift together flour, salt and soda. Beat in flour alternately with buttermilk. Add vanilla. Blend in candy and pecans. Bake in greased, floured tube pan about 1¼ hours at 350 degrees. Cool on rack 10 minutes before removing from pan.

Envy/Cakes

GATEAU DIABOLIQUE

1 ounce unsweetened chocolate
1 ounce semi-sweet chocolate
2 tablespoons water
3 eggs

Scant 1 cup sugar
½ cup flour
Dash of salt

Melt chocolates with water. Set aside. In double boiler, stir eggs and sugar until thickened. Remove from heat and continue beating until mixture cools. Blend in cooled chocolate. Sift flour with salt and fold into chocolate mixture. Bake in a greased, floured 9-inch cake pan about 45 minutes at 375 degrees.

GATEAU DIABOLIQUE FILLING

5 tablespoons sugar
2 tablespoons water
2 egg yolks, slightly beaten

1 stick butter, creamed
1 teaspoon vanilla or 1 tablespoon any liqueur

Dissolve sugar in water and boil to thread stage (265 degrees). Beat into egg yolks slowly until thick. Gradually beat in butter and add flavoring. When cake is cool, split and sandwich with filling. Frost with *Chocolate Glacé Frosting*.

NEARLY NUTRITIOUS CAKE

2 ounces unsweetened chocolate
3 tablespoons water
¼ cup sugar
1½ sticks butter, softened
2 cups sugar
4 egg yolks, slightly beaten
2 cups flour

1 teaspoon cream of tartar
½ teaspoon salt
½ teaspoon soda
3 cups milk
1½ teaspoons vanilla
4 egg whites, stiffly beaten

Melt chocolate in water. Add ¼ cup sugar. Cream butter and rest of sugar. Beat in egg yolks until light and creamy. Blend in chocolate. Sift together flour, cream of tartar, salt and soda. Add vanilla to milk. Beat in flour alternately with milk. Fold in egg whites. Bake in 3 greased, floured 9-inch cake pans 30-35 minutes, or until done, at 350 degrees. Frost with any chocolate frosting.

EDEN VALE CREAM CAKE

1½ cups graham cracker crumbs
2 tablespoons butter, melted
2 tablespoons sugar
16 ounces cream cheese, softened
1 tablespoon milk
½ cup sugar
Dash cinnamon
1 teaspoon vanilla

2 egg yolks
2 ounces semi-sweet chocolate,
   melted and cooled
2 egg whites, stiffly beaten
1 cup sour cream
1 tablespoon sugar
1 teaspoon vanilla

Blend crumbs, butter and 2 tablespoons sugar, and press into bottom of 9-inch spring-form pan. Blend cream cheese, milk, ½ cup sugar, cinnamon and 1 teaspoon vanilla. Beat in egg yolks, one at a time, and blend in chocolate. Fold in egg whites. Pour mixture onto top of crust. Bake 45 minutes at 300 degrees. Blend sour cream, 1 tablespoon sugar and 1 teaspoon vanilla and spread on top of cake. Return to oven and bake 10 minutes. Cool before removing rim of pan.

FALLEN ANGEL

10 egg whites
¼ teaspoon salt
1¼ teaspoons cream of tartar
1 cup sugar

1 teaspoon vanilla
¾ cup cake flour
4 tablespoons cocoa
¼ cup sugar

Beat egg whites with salt until frothy. Add cream of tartar and beat until stiff but not dry. Gradually beat in sugar. Fold in vanilla. Sift together dry ingredients 4 times. Gradually sift and fold flour mixture into egg whites. Bake in ungreased tube pan 30-35 minutes at 375 degrees.

CHOCOLATE CONFUSION

2 sticks butter, softened
3 cups sugar
3 eggs
3 cups flour
¼ teaspoon soda

1 teaspoon salt
1 cup sour cream
2 teaspoons vanilla
2 ounces semi-sweet chocolate,
   melted and cooled

Cream butter and sugar. Beat in eggs one at a time. Sift flour with soda and salt. Add alternately, beating well, with sour cream. Add vanilla. To one third of batter, add chocolate. Pour plain batter into greased, floured tube pan. Swirl in chocolate batter to give marbled effect. Bake about 1½ hours at 325 degrees.

SACHER TORTE

1 stick butter, softened
¾ cup powdered sugar
5 eggs, separated
4 ounces semi-sweet chocolate, melted and cooled
1 teaspoon cinnamon
¼ teaspoon cloves
2 teaspoons lemon zest (grated lemon peel)
1 cup zweiback crumbs or fine bread crumbs, toasted
1 teaspoon baking powder
¼ teaspoon salt
Apricot jam

Cream butter and sugar. Beat in egg yolks one at a time. Fold in chocolate, cinnamon, cloves and lemon zest. Beat egg whites with salt until stiff and fold them into chocolate mixture. Bake in 2 greased 8-inch pans at 325 degrees for 20-25 minutes. Cool and remove from pans. Spread bottom layer with tart apricot jam. Frost with *Creamy Chocolate Frosting*.

HAZELNUT TORTE

9 eggs
¾ cup sugar
1½ cups ground hazlenuts
¾ cup flour
¼ teaspoon salt
6 ounces chocolate chips
1 pint whipping cream, whipped
½ teaspoon vanilla
3 tablespoons powdered sugar
3 tablespoons creme de cacao

Separate eggs. Beat yolks. Add ¾ cup sugar and blend well. Add 1 cup ground nuts. Blend in flour. Beat whites with salt. Fold into first mixture. Add chocolate. Bake in 3 layers 20 minutes at 325 degrees. Cool. Flavor whipped cream with vanilla. Add powdered sugar, crème de cacao and nuts. Fill and frost the torte.

HELL WEEK CAKE

1 stick butter, softened
1 cup sugar
2 eggs
3 ounces unsweetened chocolate, melted
2 cups self-rising flour
½ teaspoon baking soda
1 cup milk
1 teaspoon vanilla
1 (14-ounce) can condensed milk

Cream butter and sugar. Beat in eggs one at a time. Blend in cooled, melted chocolate. Combine flour and soda and add alternately with milk, beating thoroughly. Add vanilla. Bake in 2 greased, floured 9-inch pans 20 minutes at 375 degrees. Boil unopened can of condensed milk 3½ hours, being careful to keep it covered with water at all times. Spread on bottom layer to form filling. Frost with a half recipe of any chocolate frosting. A dorm favorite!

Envy/Cakes

SCREWTAPE ROLL

2 eggs
½ cup plus 1 tablespoon sugar
½ cup plus 3 tablespoons self-rising flour
Few drops vanilla
½ recipe Chocolate Custard

Beat eggs and sugar until thick and creamy. Gently fold in flour. Add vanilla. Spread batter on a well-greased Swiss Roll pan, 9 x 12 x 1½ inches, and bake 7-8 minutes at 425 degrees. Turn upside down onto sugared waxed paper. Spread with *Chocolate Custard*, and roll, drawing the paper over cake and away from you. Fold paper around cake and let set a few minutes. Remove paper and cool.

WITCHES' GOLD

3 cups flour
2 cups sugar
2 teaspoons soda
½ teaspoon salt
½ teaspoon cinnamon or pumpkin pie spice
2 teaspoons baking powder
1 cup oil
2 cups pumpkin
4 eggs
1 cup pecans, chopped
6 ounces chocolate chips

Combine dry ingredients. Stir in oil and pumpkin. Beat in eggs, one at a time. Fold in nuts and chocolate chips. Bake in a greased, floured tube pan 1 hour, or until done, at 350 degrees. Good for Halloween goblins!

CHOCOLATE POUND CAKE

1 cup butter
½ cup shortening
2¾ cups sugar
5 eggs
3 cups flour
1 teaspoon baking powder
½ teaspoon salt
¾ cup cocoa
1 cup milk
2 teaspoons vanilla
½ teaspoon cinnamon

Cream butter and shortening until light and fluffy. Add the sugar gradually and blend well. Add eggs one at a time, blending well after each addition. Combine and sift all dry ingredients and add to butter and sugar alternately with milk, beginning and ending with dry ingredients. Add vanilla and cinnamon. Bake in a greased, floured tube pan at 350 degrees until done--about 1¼ hours. Pour *Chocolate Glaze* over cooled cake.

CHOCOLATE CHIFFON CAKE

2 cups self-rising flour
1¾ cups sugar
¼ cup brown sugar
½ cup corn oil
5 egg yolks
¾ cup cold water
2 teaspoons vanilla
2 ounces unsweetened chocolate, melted
7 egg whites
½ teaspoon cream of tartar

Combine flour and sugars. Make a well and add oil, egg yolks, water and vanilla. Mix thoroughly and blend in chocolate. Beat egg whites until frothy. Add cream of tartar and beat until very stiff. Gently fold chocolate mixture into egg whites. Bake in ungreased tube pan 1 hour at 325 degrees, then 15 minutes at 350 degrees. Frost with *Chocolate Glaze*.

AMARETTO CAKE

2 Devil's-Food Cake *layers*
¼ cup Amaretto
Custard from Angel Puffs
Chocolate Glaze

When cake layers are cool, split in half. Drizzle Amaretto over 3 layers, reserving one top. Sandwich together with custard cream. Glaze and chill several hours.

BLACK FOREST CAKE

1 stick butter, softened
1 cup sugar
2 eggs
1½ cups flour
½ teaspoon baking powder
½ teaspoon salt
½ cup milk
¾ cup almonds, ground
½ teaspoon vanilla
¼ teaspoon almond extract
¼ cup kirsch
Continental Cream Frosting

Cream butter and sugar. Beat in eggs one at a time and beat well. Sift together flour, baking powder and salt. Add flour alternately with milk, beating well. Blend in almonds, vanilla and almond extract. Bake in a greased, floured 9-inch cake pan for about 25 minutes at 375 degrees. When cool, split layer and drizzle half the kirsch over bottom layer and sandwich with *Continental Cream Frosting.* Drizzle remaining kirsch onto top of cake and frost. Chill overnight.

ARCHANGEL'S CAKE

1 angel food cake
Chocolate Custard
¼ cup crème de cacao or crème de menthe (optional)
½ pint whipping cream
1 tablespoon powdered sugar

Cut angel food cake into 3 layers. Drizzle liqueur on 2 layers. Sandwich layers with chocolate custard. Whip cream with sugar and frost cake. Chill 4 hours before serving.

BLACK VELVET

2 cups slivered almonds, slightly toasted
12 ounces chocolate chips
1 devil's-food cake mix
1 (3½-ounce) package instant chocolate pudding
4 eggs
1 cup sour cream
½ cup water
¼ cup oil
1 teaspoon vanilla
1 teaspoon almond extract
¼ teaspoon cinnamon

Sprinkle ½ cup almonds on bottom of greased 10-inch tube pan. Set aside rest of almonds and chocolate chips. Place remaining ingredients in mixer bowl. Beat 4 minutes. Fold in chips and almonds, then pour into pan. Bake in 350-degree oven 60-70 minutes. Cool 15 minutes and remove from pan. Serve with topping of whipped cream if desired.

MACAROON CUPCAKES

1¾ cups sugar
2 sticks butter, softened
5 eggs
2 cups flour
½ teaspoon salt
½ teaspoon vanilla plus ¼ teaspoon almond extract or 2 tablespoons Amaretto
1¼ cups coconut
6 ounces chocolate chips

Cream sugar and butter. Beat in eggs one at a time. Continue beating until fluffy. Fold in flour, salt and flavorings and blend thoroughly. Fold in coconut and chocolate chips. Line muffin pans with paper baking cups and fill ¾ full. Bake 20-25 minutes at 350 degrees. Makes 24 cupcakes.

CREAMY CHOCOLATE FROSTING

3 ounces semi-sweet chocolate
1½ sticks butter
3 tablespoons water
¾ cup sugar
6 tablespoons water
3 egg yolks, beaten until light
6 tablespoons vegetable shortening
1 teaspoon vanilla

Melt chocolate and butter in 3 tablespoons water over low heat. Set aside and cool. Boil sugar and 6 tablespoons water to thread stage (265 degrees). Beat sugar syrup slowly into egg yolks and continue beating until thick. Cool. Stir in shortening and whip until fluffy. Add vanilla and fold chocolate into cream.

CHOCOLATE CHEESE FROSTING

3 ounces cream cheese, softened
3 tablespoons butter, softened
1 tablespoon milk
2½ cups powdered sugar
1 ounce unsweetened chocolate, melted
1 teaspoon vanilla
Dash of salt

Cream together cream cheese, butter and milk. Gradually beat in sugar. Blend in chocolate, vanilla and salt.

ANGEL FLUFF FROSTING

4 tablespoons butter, softened
1½ cups powdered sugar
1 teaspoon vanilla
¼ teaspoon salt
3 ounces unsweetened chocolate, melted
2 egg whites

Cream butter and ¾ cup sugar. Add vanilla, salt and chocolate. In a separate bowl, beat egg whites, adding ¾ cup sugar till softly stiff. Fold together.

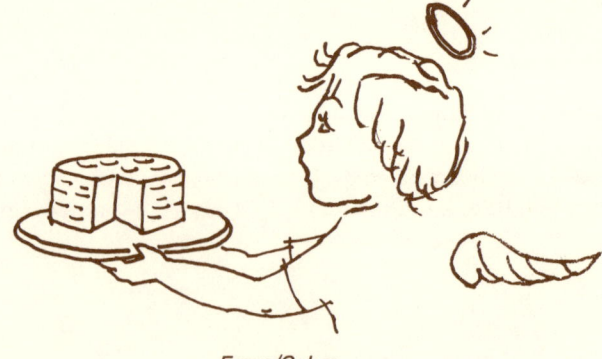

Envy/Cakes

CHOCOLATE BUTTER FROSTING

1 stick butter
2 ounces unsweetened chocolate
1 box powdered sugar
Dash of salt
6 tablespoons milk
1 teaspoon vanilla

Melt butter and chocolate. Beat in remaining ingredients.

CONTINENTAL CREAM FROSTING

½ pint whipping cream
Few drops vanilla or 1 teaspoon kirsch
2 tablespoons powdered sugar
2 ounces semi-sweet chocolate, shaved

Whip cream till firm. Blend in flavoring and sugar. Fold in chocolate.

VIENNESE CREAM FROSTING

3 ounces unsweetened chocolate
1 ounce semi-sweet chocolate
4 egg yolks
½ cup sugar
½ cup whipping cream
1 teaspoon vanilla
1 stick butter, softened

Melt chocolates in double boiler. Beat egg yolks with sugar. Blend in cream and add to chocolate. Cook, stirring constantly, until thickened. Remove from heat. Add vanilla. Gradually beat in butter.

SEVEN-MINUTE FROSTING

3 egg whites
1½ cups sugar
½ teaspoon cream of tartar
5 tablespoons cold water
Dash of salt
1 teaspoon vanilla

In top of double boiler, place whites, sugar, cream of tartar, water and salt. Beat over low heat till ingredients are well blended. Over boiling water, cook and beat until the icing holds peaks. Remove from heat and beat till it reaches spreading consistency. Do not overcook. Add vanilla.

CHOCOLATE SEVEN-MINUTE FROSTING

Break two or three ounces of unsweetened chocolate into frosting just before it is removed from the heat. Beat until chocolate melts and then remove from heat, add vanilla and continue to beat to desired consistency.

Envy/Cakes

CHOCOLATE GLACE FROSTING

1 cup powdered sugar
5 tablespoons cocoa
½ stick butter

3 tablespoons water
5 tablespoons sugar
1 teaspoon vanilla

Sift together powdered sugar and cocoa. Combine butter, water, sugar and vanilla in heavy pot and cook, stirring, over low heat to the boil. Remove from heat. Pour into sifted ingredients. Beat until smooth. Frosting will thicken as it cools. Stir occasionally while cooling. Pour over cake.

CHOCOLATE GLAZE

2 ounces semi-sweet chocolate
1 tablespoon butter

1 tablespoon milk
6 tablespoons powdered sugar

Melt chocolate and butter in milk over low heat. Blend in sugar. Pour warm glaze over cake.

FUDGE FROSTING

3 cups sugar
1 cup milk
4 ounces unsweetened chocolate
¼ cup corn syrup

Dash of salt
5 tablespoons butter
1 teaspoon vanilla

Combine sugar, milk, chocolate, corn syrup and salt and boil, stirring often, until soft ball stage (238 degrees). Remove from heat and add but do not stir in the butter and vanilla. Cool about an hour and beat until creamy.

COUNTRY FROSTING

2 cups brown sugar, firmly packed
1 cup sugar
3 ounces unsweetened chocolate

1 stick butter
1 cup light cream
1 teaspoon vanilla

Combine sugars, chocolate, butter and cream in heavy pot and cook to soft ball stage (238 degrees). Cool. Add vanilla and beat.

Envy/Cakes

SLOTH
Puddings

Puddings are very slothful. They take their own sweet time to steam, bake or chill. And if you eat too many servings--and that will be the temptation--you, too, will be slow moving and appear slothful. You have been warned. Abandon hope ye who enter this section!

Chocolate Charlotte
Black Magic
Choco-Berry Cream
Basin St. Pudding
Calypso Floating Island
Sin City à la Klare
Parson's Pudding
Sell-Your-Soul Pudding
Lady Godiva
Bavarian Cream
Mad About Mousse
Custard Sans Chocolate
Chocolate Custard
Apricot Angel Pudding
Chocolate Trifle
Simple Sin
Annwfn Rice Pudding
Pot de Crème
Quick Chocolate Soufflé
Mocha Cups
Creamy Chocolate-Celeste
Woefully Wicked Dessert

CHOCOLATE CHARLOTTE

3 cups milk
3 eggs
1¼ cups sugar
2 tablespoons flour
4 ounces semi-sweet chocolate, melted

1 tablespoon vanilla
2 tablespoons plain gelatin
1 cup warm water
1 pint whipping cream, whipped and slightly sweetened

Combine first four ingredients and cook until mixture coats spoon. Stir in melted chocolate and vanilla. Dissolve gelatin in warm water. Add to custard mixture and blend until smooth. Remove from heat and begin to cool. When mixture has thickened, fold in ½ pint of whipped cream. Line a silver bowl with Lady Fingers and pour in mixture. Garnish with other ½ pint of whipped cream. Dot with maraschino cherries, if desired.

BLACK MAGIC

2 ounces unsweetened chocolate
2 tablespoons butter
2 tablespoons water
1 cup flour
1½ teaspoons baking powder
¼ teaspoon salt
1 cup sugar

½ cup milk
1 teaspoon vanilla
¾ cup brown sugar, firmly packed
3 tablespoons cocoa
1½ cups boiling water
Vanilla ice cream

Melt chocolate and butter in water and set aside. Combine flour, baking powder, salt and sugar. Stir in milk, chocolate and vanilla. Pour into ungreased 9-inch square pan. Combine brown sugar and cocoa. Sprinkle over batter. Pour boiling water over batter. Bake about 35-40 minutes at 350 degrees. Cool slightly before cutting into squares. Top with ice cream and spoon on sauce.

CHOCO-BERRY CREAM

½ pint whipping cream
1 cup powdered sugar
Few drops vanilla
1 (10-ounce) package frozen raspberries or strawberries, thawed and drained
2 ounces semi-sweet chocolate, grated

Whip cream until fairly stiff. Beat in sugar and vanilla. Fold in berries and chocolate. Serves 6.

BASIN ST. PUDDING

2 eggs, slightly beaten
5 tablespoons sugar
Dash of salt
2 ounces semi-sweet chocolate, melted and cooled
2 tablespoons butter
1 teaspoon vanilla
2 cups milk, scalded
1¼ cups bread cubes, dried out in oven

Mix together eggs, sugar and salt. Stir in chocolate, butter and vanilla. Blend thoroughly. Slowly add milk. Pour bread cubes into buttered 1½-quart casserole and cover with custard. Place casserole in a pan of hot water in 325-degree oven and bake for about 1 hour. Spread sauce on pudding while still hot. Serves 8.

BASIN ST. SAUCE

5 tablespoons butter, softened
¾ cup sugar
1 or 2 tablespoons bourbon

Cream thoroughly butter and sugar. Blend in bourbon.

CALYPSO FLOATING ISLAND

1½ cups milk
2 tablespoons sugar
Dash of salt
3 egg yolks, slightly beaten
1 ounce semi-sweet chocolate, melted and cooled
1 teaspoon vanilla
3 egg whites
Dash of salt
6 tablespoons sugar

Scald milk and stir in 2 tablespoons sugar and dash of salt. Add a little of the milk to the egg yolks and then stir into milk. Cook in double boiler, stirring constantly, until mixture begins to thicken. Blend in chocolate and continue cooking, stirring, until thickened. Cool. Add vanilla. Pour into serving dish and chill. Set oven at 325 degrees. Beat egg whites with dash of salt until stiff and add sugar gradually, beating constantly. Put meringue on a greased pie plate and swirl top of meringue with back of a spoon. Place pie plate over a cake pan half filled with hot water. Bake about 15 minutes. Slip meringue onto custard. Serves 5 or 6.

SIN CITY A LA KLARE

12 ounces chocolate chips
4 egg yolks, beaten
1 teaspoon vanilla
½ teaspoon almond extract
4 egg whites, stiffly beaten
1½ tablespoons sugar
1 pint whipping cream, whipped
1 cup almonds, slivered
1 angel food cake
1½ cups toasted flaked coconut

Melt chocolate. Add yolks and flavorings. Remove from heat. Add sugar to beaten whites. Fold in chocolate mixture, half of the whipped cream and almonds. Line 9 x 13-inch pan with cake slices, reserving the cake for the second layer. Pour chocolate over and repeat for second layer. Garnish with remaining whipped cream and coconut. Chill overnight.

PARSON'S PUDDING

1 cup plus 4 tablespoons self-rising flour
3 tablespoons cocoa
1 stick butter, softened
¾ cup sugar
2 eggs, slightly beaten
6 tablespoons milk
½ teaspoon vanilla

Sift together flour and cocoa. Cream butter and sugar until light. Beat in eggs. Fold in cocoa mixture, milk and vanilla. Pour into a greased 2½-quart pudding bowl and cover with foil. Place in pan of water and steam 1-1½ hours. Serve warm with *Parson's Sauce.*

PARSON'S SAUCE

2 tablespoons flour
2 tablespoons cocoa
2 tablespoons butter
2 cups milk
5 tablespoons sugar
½ teaspoon vanilla

Mix flour and cocoa. Melt butter and stir in dry mixture. Gradually stir in milk. Add sugar and bring to a boil. Reduce heat and stir for 1 minute. Remove from heat and add vanilla.

SELL-YOUR-SOUL PUDDING

1 stick butter
1 cup flour
½ cup toasted pecans, chopped
½ cup toasted flake coconut
2 (6-ounce) packages instant chocolate pudding
3½ cups milk
1 cup powdered sugar
8 ounces cream cheese, softened
1 pint whipping cream
¼ cup sugar
½ teaspoon vanilla
½ teaspoon almond extract

Set aside one tablespoon pecans and coconut for decoration. Combine butter, flour, and remainder of pecans and coconut. Spread on bottom of 9 x 13-inch pan. Bake at 350 degrees 15 minutes. Remove from oven and cool. Mix instant pudding and milk. Blend sugar and cream cheese and spread on crust. Pour pudding over cream cheese. Top with whipping cream whipped with sugar and flavorings. Sprinkle on reserved toasted pecans and coconut. Refrigerate at least 4 hours.

LADY GODIVA

12 ounces milk chocolate
½ cup water
6 eggs
3 tablespoons orange liqueur
Whipped cream

Place chocolate and water in top of double boiler. Melt. Separate eggs and beat yolks. Add chocolate to yolks and continue beating. Beat whites until stiff. Fold in liqueur. Combine whites and chocolate mixture. Pour into souffle dish and refrigerate until set, preferably overnight. Garnish with whipped cream.

Sloth/Puddings

BAVARIAN CREAM

1 tablespoon plain gelatin
3 tablespoons tepid water
1½ cups milk
2 ounces semi-sweet chocolate
¼ cup sugar

Dash of salt
1 teaspoon vanilla
1 teaspoon almond extract
½ pint whipping cream
6-8 Lady Fingers

Dissolve gelatin in water and set aside. Bring milk to a near boil. Shave 1 tablespoon chocolate and set aside. Add rest of chocolate, sugar and salt to milk. Stir in gelatin and set in refrigerator. When the mixture has begun to thicken, add flavorings and beat until mixture is light and fluffy. Whip cream and fold into gelatin mixture. Pour into spring-form pan in layers alternating with Lady Fingers, ending with whipped cream mixture. Decorate with shaved chocolate.

MAD ABOUT MOUSSE

4 egg yolks
4 eggs
¼ teaspoon salt
12 ounces semi-sweet chocolate, melted

2 tablespoons powdered sugar
2 teaspoons vanilla or 2 tablespoons brandy or orange liqueur
½ pint whipping cream

Beat egg yolks, eggs and salt till light. Beat in cooled chocolate, sugar and flavoring. Add cream and continue beating until mixture is smooth and thick. Turn into serving dish and chill thoroughly. Serves 8.

Sloth/Puddings

CUSTARD SANS CHOCOLATE

3 tablespoons sugar
1 tablespoon flour
2 eggs, slightly beaten

2 cups milk, scalded
½ teaspoon vanilla

Combine sugar and flour. Beat into eggs. Add to scalded milk in double boiler and cook, stirring often until thickened. Add vanilla. Cool.

CHOCOLATE CUSTARD

Follow recipe for *Custard Sans Chocolate* and beat 2 ounces semi-sweet chocolate, melted and cooled, into egg mixture.

APRICOT ANGEL PUDDING

Famous Chocolate Wafers
Custard Sans Chocolate

1 small can apricots, drained

Line dish with chocolate wafers. Spread on half the custard, then arrange apricots on custard. Repeat layers. Cover with foil and chill throughly.

CHOCOLATE TRIFLE

2 eggs
½ cup sugar
½ cup self-rising flour
½ teaspoon vanilla
Raspberry jam

¼ cup crème de cacao
Chocolate Custard
½ cup whipping cream, whipped
    and slightly sweetened
¼ cup almonds, slivered

Beat eggs till light. Beat in sugar. Fold in flour a little at a time. Add vanilla. Bake in greased, floured 8-inch pan at 350 degrees for 25 minutes. When cool, line a souffle dish with cake. Spread cake with raspberry jam. Drizzle on liqueur. Cover with custard and chill thoroughly. Top with whipped cream and almonds.

SIMPLE SIN

1 tablespoon cornstarch
¼ cup milk
1¾ cups milk, scalded
¾ cup sugar
¼ cup brown sugar, firmly packed
2 ounces unsweetened chocolate, melted
Dash of salt
3 egg yolks, slightly beaten
1 teaspoon vanilla
3 egg whites
6 tablespoons sugar
Raspberry jam

Dissolve cornstarch in ¼ cup milk. Add cornstarch, sugars, chocolate and salt to milk in double boiler. Cook, stirring, until thickened. Blend in egg yolks. Add vanilla. Pour into a casserole. Beat egg whites till stiff, gradually adding sugar. Gently spoon a little raspberry jam over custard. Spread on meringue. Place casserole in a pan half filled with warm water. Bake until meringue begins to brown at 300 degrees, about 10 minutes.

ANNWFN RICE PUDDING

2 cups cooked rice
1 cup milk
½ cup sugar
1 egg, slightly beaten
1 tablespoon butter
½ teaspoon cinnamon
½ cup chocolate chips
1 teaspoon vanilla

Heat rice, milk and sugar over low heat. Add a little of mixture to beaten egg and stir into rice, blending thoroughly. Cook, stirring, until mixture thickens. Remove from heat and add butter, cinnamon and vanilla. Fold in chocolate chips. Pour into 6 custard cups. Top with whipped cream, if desired.

POT DE CREME

2 cups milk, warmed
1 pound semi-sweet chocolate
6 egg yolks, beaten
1 teaspoon vanilla or 2 tablespoons curaçao or rum

Warm milk over low heat. Add chocolate and stir till mixture reaches boiling point. Remove from heat. Blend thoroughly into egg yolks. Strain. Add flavoring and pour into little *pots* or custard cups or demi-tasse cups. Chill thoroughly. May be served with whipped cream. Serves 8.

QUICK CHOCOLATE SOUFFLE

8 egg whites
½ cup Chocolate Syrup
1 teaspoon vanilla
1 teaspoon almond extract

Preheat oven to 350 degrees. Beat whites until stiff. Fold in syrup gently. Add flavorings. Turn into soufflé pan. Set in hot water and place in oven. Reduce heat to 325 degrees. Bake till crust forms. Garnish with whipped cream, if desired.

MOCHA CUPS

½ cup boiling water
4 teaspoons instant coffee
½ cup milk
1 egg, slightly beaten
10 large marshmallows
½ teaspoon gelatin
2 tablespoons cold water
½ pint whipping cream
1 tablespoon powdered sugar
4 Chocolate Cases
½ ounce semi-sweet chocolate, shaved

Stir instant coffee into boiling water and add milk. Spoon a small portion of the mixture into beaten egg and blend. Add egg mixture to coffee, stirring to blend well. Add marshmallows and cook, stirring, over moderate heat until marshmallows are melted and mixture is slightly thickened. Add half of the unwhipped cream and the gelatin which has been softened in cold water and blend well. Pour into *Chocolate Cases*. Whip remainder of cream with 1 tablespoon powdered sugar. Top each cup with whipped cream and decorate with shaved chocolate.

CREAMY CHOCOLATE-CELESTE

7 ounces semi-sweet chocolate
½ ounce unsweetened chocolate
2 tablespoons butter
2 tablespoons brandy
2 eggs, separated
Dash of salt
1 pint whipping cream

Melt chocolates and butter in double boiler. Blend. Remove from heat. Stir in brandy, yolks and salt. Return to heat and stir for one or two minutes. When chocolate mixture has cooled slightly, fold in stiffly beaten whites. Whip cream and fold in. Place in individual dessert ramekins. Top with chopped nuts, if desired.

WOEFULLY WICKED DESSERT

2 cups milk
3 ounces semi-sweet chocolate, grated
3 egg yolks, well-beaten
½ pint whipping cream
1 tablespoon powdered sugar
2 tablespoons brandy
1 teaspoon vanilla

Scald milk over low heat. Add chocolate and stir until smooth. Stir a little of the mixture into the egg yolks. Gradually stir eggs into mixture and heat, stirring, until thick. Cool. Whip cream until firm then whip in sugar. Add brandy and vanilla. Fold cooled chocolate mixture into the whipped cream. Pour into custard cups and chill thoroughly. Serves 8.

Sloth/Puddings

PRIDE
Beverages

"Proud as punch" you will be to serve any of these chocolate drinks. "Pride goeth before a fall," as the saying goes. Some of the drinks, if taken in excess, will prove the saying true. But St. Nick and St. Patrick and a few Puritans are here to fight the demons and diablos for you.

Hot Chocolate
Coffee St. Patrick
Café Diable
Cappucino
Parisian Folly
Café Belgique
Puritans' Punch
Choco-Mocha Milk
Old St. Nick
Chocolate Milk Punch
Inca Inc
Lethe
Summer Sin
Caesar
Alexander
London Cocktail
Backslider
Scipio
Grasshopper
D.O.M.
Cool Chocolate Soda

HOT CHOCOLATE

2 ounces semi-sweet chocolate
1 cup water
Dash of salt

Few drops of vanilla
3 cups warm milk

Heat chocolate in water with salt until chocolate is blended. Boil 1 minute, stirring constantly. Add vanilla. Gradually add warm milk. Beat until frothy. Makes 5 cups.

COFFEE ST. PATRICK

1 cup hot black coffee
1½ ounces Irish whisky
1 teaspoon sugar

2 tablespoons whipped cream, sweetened
Grated semi-sweet chocolate

Combine coffee, whisky and sugar. Pour into a glass, not a cup, and top with whipped cream. Sprinkle a little chocolate on top of cream.

CAFE DIABLE

1½ cups brandy
2 tablespoons sugar
1 teaspoon cocoa

Piece of orange peel
2 sticks cinnamon
6 cups strong coffee

Combine all ingredients except coffee. Heat and flame. Add flame mixture to coffee. Serve in cups immediately. Whipped cream or very heavy whipping cream, unwhipped, may be floated on each filled cup.

CAPPUCINO

2 teaspoons instant coffee
2 tablespoons instant hot chocolate mix

2 cups boiling water
2 tablespoons brandy
Whipped cream

Combine all ingredients. Pour into small cups. Top with whipped cream. Serves 5-6.

PARISIAN FOLLY

4 ounces semi-sweet chocolate
¼ cup corn syrup
Dash of salt
1 teaspoon vanilla
½ pint whipping cream, whipped
1 quart milk

Melt chocolate in corn syrup over low heat. Stir in salt and vanilla. Cool. Fold into whipped cream and spoon into teacups. Scald milk and pour over cream. Serves 10.

CAFE BELGIQUE

2 cups hot coffee
2 cups hot chocolate
Whipped cream, slightly sweetened

Combine coffee and chocolate and top with whipped cream.

PURITANS' PUNCH

2 quarts chocolate ice cream or sherbet
1 gallon hot strong coffee
1 large bottle soda water

Blend 1½ quarts ice cream into hot coffee. Chill until time to serve. Add soda water and float ½ quart ice cream. When serving, spoon a little ice cream into each cup. About 4 dozen cups.

CHOCO-MOCHA MILK

1 cup boiling water
4 tablespoons instant coffee
2 tablespoons sugar
2 tablespoons Kahlua
1 quart milk
2 teaspoons vanilla
1 pint chocolate ice cream
1 pint coffee ice cream
Whipped cream
Cinnamon
Nutmeg

Combine boiling water, instant coffee and sugar. Cool and add Kahlua. Mix with milk and vanilla. Blend ice cream into milk mixture. Serve garnished with whipped cream and dash of cinnamon and nutmeg.

OLD ST. NICK

4 egg yolks, beaten
½ cup Chocolate Syrup
2 cups light cream
2 cups milk
1 pint bourbon
1 jigger rum
4 egg whites, stiffly beaten but not dry
Nutmeg

Beat egg yolks till light and creamy. Beat in chocolate syrup, cream and milk. Add bourbon and rum. Fold in egg whites and chill thoroughly. To serve, pour into punch cups and grate nutmeg on top. About 10 cups.

CHOCOLATE MILK PUNCH

1 cup cold milk
2 tablespoons chocolate syrup
1 jigger bourbon
2 tablespoons crushed ice
Nutmeg

Pour all ingredients except nutmeg into blender and blend a few seconds. Serve with grated nutmeg sprinkled over top.

INCA ICE

1 teaspoon gelatin
2 tablespoons water
2 cups strong coffee
½ cup sugar
3 cups milk
1 pint chocolate ice cream
Cinnamon

Soften gelatin in water. Bring coffee and sugar to the boil. Remove from heat. Stir in gelatin until dissolved. Freeze in freezer tray until firm, stirring occasionally. Turn into mixer or processor and blend in milk. Pour into glasses, add scoop of chocolate ice cream, and sprinkle cinnamon on top.

LETHE

1 ounce gin
½ ounce crème de cacao
Crushed ice

Combine ingredients in a shaker and shake well.

SUMMER SIN

1 part crème de cacao
2 parts vodka

Crushed ice
Gardenia petals

Blend crème de cacao, vodka and ice. Float gardenia petals.

CAESAR

½ ounce crème de cacao
½ ounce Sambuca Romano
½ ounce light cream

¼ cup crushed ice
Lemon zest (strips of lemon peel)

Blend liqueurs, cream and ice. Pour into chilled glass and garnish with a couple of lemon strips.

ALEXANDER

½ ounce brandy
½ ounce crème de cacao

½ ounce light cream
¼ cup crushed ice

Blend ingredients and serve in chilled glass.

LONDON COCKTAIL

1 egg yolk, slightly whipped
3 ounces port wine
1 ounce chartreuse

1 teaspoon semi-sweet chocolate, grated
1 jigger crushed ice

In a shaker, combine egg yolk, port, chartreuse and chocolate and shake well. Strain over ice in glass.

BACKSLIDER

1 part Kahlua
1 part crème de cacao
Dash bitters (optional)

Crushed ice
Soda water

Blend liqueurs with ice. Fill glass with soda water.

SCIPIO

½ ounce Amaretto
½ ounce crème de cacao
½ ounce light cream
¼ cup crushed ice

Blend ingredients and serve in chilled glass.

GRASSHOPPER

½ ounce crème de cacao
½ ounce crème de menthe
½ ounce light cream
¼ cup crushed ice

Blend ingredients and pour into chilled glass.

D.O.M.

½ ounce creme de cacao, chilled   Champagne, chilled

Pour crème de cacao into chilled champagne glass and fill with champagne.

COOL CHOCOLATE SODA

5 mint leaves, chopped
1 ounce crème de cacao
¼ cup crushed ice
Soda water

Put mint leaves into glass. Blend liqueur and ice. Pour onto leaves and add soda.

INDEX

BEVERAGES

Alexander, 75
Backslider, 75
Caesar, 75
Café Belgique, 73
Café Diablo, 72
Cappucino, 72
Chocolate Milk Punch, 74
Choco-Mocha Milk, 73
Coffee St. Patrick, 72
Cool Chocolate Soda, 76
D.O.M., 76
Grasshopper, 76
Hot Chocolate, 72
Inca Ice, 74
Lethe, 74
London Cocktail, 75
Old St. Nick, 74
Parisian Folly, 73
Puritans' Punch, 73
Scipio, 76
Summer Sin, 75

CAKES

Amaretto Cake, 56
Angel Fluff Frosting, 58
Archangel's Cake, 57
Black Forest Cake, 56
Black Velvet, 57
Chocolate Butter Frosting, 59
Chocolate Chiffon Cake, 56
Chocolate Confusion, 53
Chocolate Cream Frosting, 58
Chocolate Glacé Frosting, 60
Chocolate Glaze, 60
Chocolate Myracle, 48
Chocolate Pound Cake, 55
Chocolate Seven-Minute Frosting, 59
Continental Cream Frosting, 59
Country Frosting, 60
Creamy Chocolate Frosting, 58
Devil's-Food Cake, 46
Eden Vale Cream Cake, 53
Fallen Angel, 53
Fat City, 51
Fat City Frosting, 51
Fat City Topping, 51
Fudge Fantasy Cake, 46
Fudge Frosting, 60
Gateau Diabolique, 52
Gateau Diabolique Filling, 52
German Sweet Chocolate Cake, 49
German Sweet Chocolate Frosting, 49
Hazelnut Torte, 54
Hell Week Cake, 54
Hershey Bar Cake, 50
Hershey Bar Frosting, 50
"Looking for Mr. Goodbar" Cake, 50
Macaroon Cupcakes, 57
Milky Way Cake, 51
Myracle Topping, 48
Nearly Nutritious Cake, 52
Persephone's Cake, 46
Sacher Torte, 54
Screwtape Roll, 55
Seven-Minute Frosting, 59
Seventh Heaven Cake, 47

Seventh Heaven Frosting, 47
Sheer Perfidy, 47
Tower of Babel Cake, 49
Vicarage Frosting, 48
Vicarage Tea Cake, 48
Viennese Cream Frosting, 59
Witches' Gold, 55

CANDY

Almost Divinity, 10
Beelzebub's Baubles, 11
Bitter Sweet Fruit, 11
British Sins, 15
Cerberus' Chews, 14
Charon's Reward, 14
Chocolate Persuasion Pralines, 10
Chocolate Yule Log, 16
Cool Turkish Delight, 15
Foolish Virgins, 12
Fudge Francesca, 13
Heavenly Happening, 10
Hershey Bar Fudge, 12
Imps, 16
John Minary's Tranquilizers, 15
Little Devils, 16
Parish House Fudge, 12
Pitch Fork Fudge, 11
Rich Man's Fudge, 13
White Chocolate Dip, 13
White Rings 'n Things, 14

COOKIES

Beatrice's Fingers, 34
Bonnie Brownies, 32
Caena Cookies, 33
Chocolate Styx, 36
Chocolate Wings, 36
Cleopatras, 33
Cocoacoons, 31
Final Frosting, 32
Forbidden Kisses, 31
Gambler's Chips, 30
Gambler's Filling, 30
Gwen's Health Food, 34
Intermediate Frosting, 32
Jan's Sin Squares, 31
Lazy Day Cookies, 35
Near Fatal Drops, 36
Neglected Nuggets, 30
Peanut Butter Hexes, 34
Pegged Stage Planks, 30
Sirens, 35
Snap Judgments, 33
Spanish Squares, 35
Top Hats, 32

ICE CREAM

Blazing Bananas, 42
Chocolate Bombe, 44
Cherries Jubilee de Cacao, 42
Chocolate Cases, 40
Chocolate Envy, 38
Chocolate Sherbet, 39
Chocolate Syrup, 41
Cocoa Syrup, 41
Coffee Confection, 38
Fire 'n Ice Cream, 38
Flaming Black Forest Cake, 43
Frozen Fire, 39
Heaven-Can-Wait Pie, 41
Hot Fudge Royal Sauce, 40
Hot Fudge Sauce, 40
Hot Stuff!, 40
Klondike Demon, 43
Meringue Glacé, 44
Mint Frappé, 44
Parfait Apollo, 43
Preacher's Dessert, 44
Refrigerator Ice Cream, 38
Sunday Soda, 41
Tortoni Santa Lucia, 42

PASTRY

Angel Pie, 19
Angel Puffs and Éclairs, 24
Billionaire Pie, 21
Bishop's Bread, 27
Black Demon Pie, 18
Black Forest Pie, 22
Boston Cream Filling, 20
Boston Cream Frosting, 20
Boston Cream Pie, 20
Chocolate Chess Pie, 21
Chocolate Cream Pie, 19
Chocolate Pie Crust, 23
Chocolate Wafer Crust, 25
Ciacco's Choco-Mocha Pie, 20
Cloud Nine Chiffon Pie, 21
Creation Coffee Cake, 26
Creation Topping, 26
Crêpes Lucifer, 27
Crooked Halos, 28
Double Trouble Waffles, 28
Flaming Lucifer Sauce, 27
Fudge Pie, 18
Ginger Snap Crust, 18
Good Intentions Pie, 25
Graham Cracker Crust, 22
Grasshopper Pie, 22
Hershey Bar Crust, 23
Hershey Bar Pie, 23
Lucifer Filling, 27
Meringue St. Pamela, 24
Pandora's Boxes, 28
Persian Pastries, 26
St. Pamela Filling, 24
Scarlett's Pecan Pie, 23

PUDDINGS

Annwfn Rice Pudding, 68
Apricot Angel Pudding, 67
Basin St. Pudding, 63
Basin St. Sauce, 63
Bavarian Cream, 66
Black Magic, 62
Calypso Floating Island, 63
Choco-Berry Cream, 62
Chocolate Charlotte, 62
Chocolate Custard, 67
Chocolate Trifle, 67
Creamy Chocolate-Celeste, 69
Custard Sans Chocolate, 67
Lady Godiva, 65
Mad About Mousse, 66
Mocha Cups, 69
Quick Chocolate Soufflé, 69
Parson's Pudding, 64
Parson's Sauce, 64
Pot de Crème, 68
Sell-Your-Soul Pudding, 65
Simple Sin, 68
Sin City à la Klare, 64
Woefully Wicked Dessert, 70

The Quail Ridge Press Cookbook Series:

The Country Mouse $5.95
The Twelve Days of Christmas Cookbook $5.95
The Seven Chocolate Sins $5.95
A Salad A Day $5.95
Hors D'Oeuvres Everybody Loves $5.95
Quickies for Singles $5.95
The Little Gumbo Book $6.95
Best of the Best from Louisiana $12.95
Best of the Best from Texas $14.95
Best of the Best from Florida $12.95
Best of the Best from Mississippi $12.95
Best of the Best from Tennessee $12.95

Send check or money order or VISA/MasterCard number with expiration date to:

QUAIL RIDGE PRESS
P. O. Box 123
Brandon, MS 39042

Please add $1.50 postage and handling for first book, $0.50 per additional book. Gift wrap with enclosed card no extra charge. Mississippi residents add 6% sales tax.